The Letter to the Romans

OneBook.
DAILY-WEEKLY

The Letter to the Romans

Ben Witherington III

 Seedbed

Printed in the United States of America

Cover design by Nlkabrik Design
Page design by PerfecType

Witherington, Ben, III, 1951-
The letter to the Romans / Ben Witherington III. – Franklin, Tennessee : Seedbed Publishing, ©2016.

x, 166 ; cm. + 1 videodisc – (OneBook. Daily-weekly)

Includes bibliographical references.
ISBN 9781628241822 (paperback: alk. paper)
ISBN 978-1-62824-264-5 (Mobi)
ISBN 978-1-62824-265-2 (ePub)
ISBN 978-1-62824-266-9 (uPDF)
ISBN 9781628243086 (videodisc)

1. Bible. Romans -- Textbooks. 2. Bible. Romans -- Study and teaching. 3. Bible. Romans -- Commentaries. I. Title.

BS2665.55.W574 2016   227/.10071   2016932601

SEEDBED PUBLISHING
Franklin, Tennessee
seedbed.com

CONTENTS

WELCOME TO THE ONEBOOK DAILY-WEEKLY

John Wesley, in a letter to one of his leaders, penned the following:

> O begin! Fix some part of every day for private exercises. You may acquire the taste which you have not: what is tedious at first, will afterwards be pleasant.
>
> Whether you like it or not, read and pray daily. It is for your life; there is no other way; else you will be a trifler all your days. . . . Do justice to your own soul; give it time and means to grow. Do not starve yourself any longer. Take up your cross and be a Christian altogether.

Rarely are our lives most shaped by our biggest ambitions and highest aspirations. Rather, our lives are most shaped, for better or for worse, by those small things we do every single day.

At Seedbed, our biggest ambition and highest aspiration is to resource the followers of Jesus to become lovers and doers of the Word of God every single day, to become people of One Book.

To that end, we have created the OneBook Daily-Weekly. First, it's important to understand what this is not: warm and fuzzy, sentimental devotions. If you engage the Daily-Weekly for any length of time, you will learn the Word of God. You will grow profoundly in your love for God, and you will become a passionate lover of people.

How does the Daily-Weekly work?

Daily. As the name implies, every day invites a short but substantive engagement with the Bible. Five days a week you will read a passage of Scripture followed by a short segment of teaching and closing with a question for reflection and self-examination. On the sixth day, you will review and reflect on the previous five days.

Weekly. Each week, on the seventh day, find a way to gather with at least one other person doing the study. Pursue the weekly guidance for gathering.

Share learning, insight, encouragement, and most important, how the Holy Spirit is working in your lives.

That's it. When the twelve weeks are done, we will be ready with twelve more. Four times a year we will release a new edition of the Daily-Weekly. Over time, those who pursue this course of learning will develop a rich library of Bible learning resources for the long haul. Following is the plan for how we will work our way through the Bible.

The Gospels: Twelve weeks of the year the Daily-Weekly will delve into one of the Gospels, either in a broad overview or through a deep dive into a more focused segment of the text.

The Epistles: Twelve weeks of the year the Daily-Weekly will explore one of the letters, sermons, or the Acts of the Apostles that make up the rest of the New Testament.

The Wisdom Writings: Twelve weeks of the year the Daily-Weekly will lead us into some part of the Psalms, Proverbs, or prophetic writings.

The Old Testament: Twelve weeks of the year the Daily-Weekly will engage with some portion of the Books of Moses (Genesis–Deuteronomy), the historical books, or other writings from the Old Testament.

If you are looking for a substantive study to learn Scripture through a steadfast method, look no further.

WEEK ONE

Romans 1:1–17

Longing to See You

INTRODUCTION

At the outset of Paul's letter to the Romans we have a mixture of epistolary (letter) and rhetorical elements. Ancient letters would normally begin with the name of the addresser rather than the addressee, and then the name of the audience of the letter. In addition, there was normally a brief, perfunctory greeting, and possibly a brief health wish (i.e., "hope you are doing well") followed by the main substance of the letter. Paul has modified this format to suit his rhetorical and theological purposes. It is an interesting exercise to compare and contrast the various openings of Paul's letters not only with other ancient letters, but more particularly with Paul's other letters. In fact, there are various things that are salient when one makes such a comparison, as we shall see.

Opening remarks are always important for understanding a crucial communication and this is certainly true when it comes to as complex a discourse as Romans. Here Paul will: (1) introduce himself to a largely new audience as both a servant and an apostle; (2) indicate who Jesus is both in the flesh and by the Spirit; (3) indicate he has been praying for them and intends to come to see them; (4) indicate what the essence of the gospel of God is; and (5) indicate the benefits of embracing such good news. All of this comes by way of preparation for Paul finally visiting Rome. This is something he has often longed to do, and even planned to do, but his plans heretofore had been thwarted. In a sense then, this discourse is the wake-up call to the audience that Paul is finally coming, and they need to get ready. Partly, Paul wants them to begin to prepare not merely to receive him, but as Romans 15:24 will make

POSSESSIVE

1

clear, to "have [them] assist [him] on [his] journey there." This is a technical phrase, which means to provide material and monetary resources for his journey to his next mission field—Spain. While we know Paul got to Rome, we honestly do not know if he ever made it to Spain.

ONE

Introductions

N/V

Romans 1:1–7 *Paul, a servant of Christ Jesus, called to be an apostle and set apart for the gospel of God—²the gospel he promised beforehand through his prophets in the Holy Scriptures ³regarding his Son, who as to his earthly life was a descendant of David, ⁴and who through the Spirit of holiness was appointed the Son of God in power by his resurrection from the dead: Jesus Christ our Lord. ⁵Through him we received grace and apostleship to call all the Gentiles to the obedience that comes from faith for his name's sake. ⁶And you also are among those Gentiles who are called to belong to Jesus Christ.*

⁷ To all in Rome who are loved by God and called to be his holy people:
Grace and peace to you from God our Father and from the Lord Jesus Christ.

Understanding the Word. In the first place, Paul does not lead with the fact that he is an apostle, much less that he is this audience's apostle. He leads with the affirmation that he is a servant of God. This term "servant" is, in fact, what the prophets of old were often called (see Jeremiah 44:4) and, of course, we have the Suffering Servant in Isaiah 53. The term, then, is not randomly chosen by Paul. Notice, as well, that Paul does not say, "I am your apostle." While Paul was not famous for his subtlety, here he is being careful at the outset of the document so that he might establish good rapport with the audience—an audience he had not visited or converted and mostly did not know. Furthermore, verse 2 shows that Paul was thinking about the prophets here at the outset as he says that the "gospel [good news] of God" was promised beforehand through the prophets. Usually Paul refers to the gospel of Jesus Christ, but here he refers to the gospel of God, and perhaps with good reason. Paul believes, as he will say in Romans 4, that the gospel was pre-preached to Abraham—the good news of how, if one trusted the true God, one's faith could be reckoned as righteousness, or in other words, could give one right standing with God. But, of course,

Paul also knew that Jesus, God's Son, did not come on the human stage until "the time had fully come" (see Galatians 4:4). Hence, in Paul's view it was God's gospel, before it became more specifically the gospel about Jesus. The reason for stressing this is because Paul will go on to say that this good news was for the Jew first, long before it was for Gentiles like those in Rome.

Notice, as well, that Paul goes on to stress that Jesus was of Davidic descent, something that elsewhere in his letters he barely mentions. The emphasis is on the Jewishness of Jesus (see also Romans 9) for the very good reason that he must go on and argue in Romans 9–11 that God has not forsaken his first chosen people. This is perhaps what many anti-Semitic Gentiles might have assumed if they had swallowed the rhetoric of the emperor about the Romans now being the favored people of the gods.

Verse 4 is important and needs to be translated carefully as Paul does not think that Jesus became the Son of God at the resurrection. The proper translation of the Greek would be something like "indicated" or "vindicated" "the Son of God in power." Paul clearly believes (see Galatians 4:4) that Jesus was God's Son when he was born of a woman. Indeed, he believes Jesus was God's Son from before the creation of the universe (see Philippians 2:5–11)! The resurrection, however, did two things: (1) it indicated and vindicated that Jesus was indeed the Son of God despite being crucified; and (2) it was at the resurrection that Jesus became the Son of God in power, became the risen Lord. Previously he had been the Son of God in weakness and vulnerability, but after the resurrection he was immune to disease, decay, and death, suffering and sin.

Paul then indicates that it was through this same Jesus that he was called to be an apostle to the Gentiles unto the aim of producing "the obedience that comes from faith." He also reminds the audience they are among those Gentiles whom God has called to this high calling to belong to Jesus. Scholars have long debated what the phrase "obedience that comes from faith" means. Does it suggest faith is a form of obedience? Well, of course, trusting in God is a form of doing what God wants, to be sure. But it is more likely he is talking about an obedience that flows from faith, as we shall see. The Gentiles in Rome are loved by God and called to belong to him, and be his holy people, along with Jewish followers of Jesus. All of this is much more elaborate than any opening salvo one finds in a contemporary ancient secular letter, but that is because Paul is not just following epistolary conventions, he also has rhetorical purposes here to set up the discourse which follows.

In the second half of verse 7 we finally have the proper greeting, and it is a typical Pauline one. By that I mean it involves two terms—"grace and peace." The typical ancient opening Greek greeting was simply the word "greeting." Interestingly, the term *charis*, which we translate "grace," is a variant of the Greek word for greeting. And, of course, "peace" or "shalom" is the standard Jewish greeting, so Paul is greeting his audience in ways that would suit first Gentiles and then Jews in his audience. Perhaps the "grace" greeting comes first because Paul, speaking as the apostle to the Gentiles, is mainly addressing Gentiles.

1. Why is he less direct in asserting his authority in this letter than in other Pauline letters?

2. What is the point of stressing both Jesus' Jewish descent and his new role as risen Lord since his death and resurrection?

3. Paul introduces himself to his audience as "servant of God" rather than "apostle." If you were to introduce yourself without a title (more at the level of identity), how would you do it? (i.e., Who are you?)

TWO

Establishing Rapport

Romans 1:8–10 RSV *First, I thank my God through Jesus Christ for all of you, because your faith is proclaimed in all the world. ⁹For God is my witness, whom I serve with my spirit in the gospel of his Son, that without ceasing I mention you always in my prayers, ¹⁰asking that somehow by God's will I may now at last succeed in coming to you.*

Understanding the Word. The exordium proper, or opening remarks that prepare for the argument which follows, can be found in verses 8–10 and it takes the form of a prayer report. Paul says he thanks God for the audience's faith, which is well known in the Christian communities throughout the entire empire. This may be a bit of rhetorical hyperbole, but that was appropriate in the exordium, where the goal was to make the audience receptive to the discourse that was about to follow. First the speaker must establish his ethos—his authority and right to address the audience—and he has done this in verses 1–7. Then he must establish rapport with the audience to make them open to hear what is to follow, and this he does in verses 8–10. Paul indicates he fervently and constantly prays for the Roman Christians, and then finally he indicates he has long wanted to visit them. This leads directly to the *narratio,* or the narration, of facts relevant to the coming discourse.

1. Why do you think Paul tells the audience what he has been praying about for them, rather than simply offering a prayer at this point in the letter?

2. What does Paul single out as the outstanding feature of the audience that many other Christians already had heard about, even if they lived a great distance away?

3. As you read this text today, who are you remembering in your prayers?

THREE

A Narration of Relevant Facts

Romans 1:11–15 RSV *For I long to see you, that I may impart to you some spiritual gift to strengthen you,* [12]*that is, that we may be mutually encouraged by each other's faith, both yours and mine.* [13]*I want you to know, brethren, that I have often intended to come to you (but thus far have been prevented), in order that I may reap some harvest among you as well as among the rest of the Gentiles.* [14]*I am under obligation both to Greeks and to barbarians, both to the wise and to the foolish:* [15]*so I am eager to preach the gospel to you also who are in Rome.*

Understanding the Word. The narratio stretches from verses 11–15 and it is very interesting to see the sort of tap dance Paul does in these verses, carefully tiptoeing around the fact that while he is the apostle to the Gentiles, he has not yet established himself as the apostle of this particular largely Gentile audience and has not even yet visited them! Thus Paul first says, quite honestly, that he longs to come to them to impart some spiritual wisdom to strengthen their faith. But then he realizes this might seem too direct an assertion of his role as their apostle, so he backtracks and says that what he means is he longs to come so that there could be some mutual sharing of benefit between Paul and this audience. Paul says that many times he had thought and purposed to come to Rome, but his plans up to the writing of this document had always been thwarted. (He does not say here by whom, but in Acts it is God's Spirit that does not permit Paul to go, for instance, to Ephesus in Asia or into Bithynia when he wants to do so. See Acts 16:6–7). Paul nonetheless comes clean at the end of the narratio as to his main purpose for coming to Rome: that he might convert some more Gentiles, and add to the Christian harvest of such folk that were already there.

As I said, this is a delicate dance between asserting authority, and recognizing that the audience does not yet recognize Paul as their apostle. This is the kind of rhetoric one uses in first-order moral discourse—the opening address to a new audience. Notice that Paul says he has an obligation to both Greeks and non-Greeks. It is interesting that Paul chooses here and immediately hereafter, to use the more specific term "Greek" rather than "Gentile" (cf. verses 14 and 16). Here Greek is contrasted with the non-Greek speaker or "barbarian." The Greek term *barbaros* from which we get the word *barbarian* actually means someone who could not speak Greek. In verse 16, however, the contrast is between Jew and Greek. Paul's point is that he is obligated to evangelize all sorts of people, including all sorts of Gentiles, both Greek-speaking and non-Greek-speaking. But as for the gospel itself, it is for the Jew first, and also for the Greek speakers!

1. Why do you think Paul had been prevented from coming to Rome before the writing of this letter?

2. Does Paul view himself as simply the apostle to the Gentiles?

3. Paul has been sensitive to not assert too much authority in his opening address. What might you personally learn from Paul in his tactful approach to this new audience?

FOUR

The Thesis Statement (Part I)

Romans 1:16 *For I am not ashamed of the gospel, because it is the power of God that brings salvation to everyone who believes: first to the Jew, then to the Gentile.*

Understanding the Word. Then finally we come to verses 16–17, which are the *propositio*, or thesis statement, of this entire Roman discourse. It will require some close attention as the major theme of what follows is announced here. It is interesting that this thesis statement begins with a remark about what Paul is not ashamed of: the gospel. Why does he put it this way? Likely it is because of the content of this good news message, namely that a Jewish crucified manual worker from Galilee had been raised from the dead and was now the risen Lord of all! Many Gentiles would have thought that suggesting a Jew might be a world savior was laughable if not shameful. But more, certainly many more, perhaps most Gentiles' instinctive reaction to the idea of a crucified man being the savior was a shameful and ridiculous notion. Crucifixion was the most shameful way to die in antiquity, and no one thought it had any redeeming value. Thus it is that Paul says he is not ashamed of this message, and proclaims it boldly.

Why is he not ashamed? Because in fact this message has power, life-changing power, power to save "everyone who believes," the Jew first, and Greeks as well. The emphasis on the word translated here as "everyone" will be echoed in various places later in the discourse, for instance in Romans 6:10. Jesus did not come to die for and to redeem just some prechosen elect group of people, whether Jewish or Gentile. He came to die for all, and salvation comes to all who believe, without prescreening. This is precisely why this message is good news for all persons with whom Paul shares the message.

1. Why does Paul start by telling the audience what he is *not* ashamed of?

2. What might have been seen as shameful about the gospel message?

3. Have you ever been ashamed of being a Christ-follower? What was the source of that shame?

FIVE

The Thesis Statement (Part II)

Romans 1:17 *For in the gospel the righteousness of God is revealed—a righteousness that is by faith from first to last, just as it is written: "The righteous will live by faith."*

Understanding the Word. Verse 17 is a controversial and much-debated verse so we will unpack it carefully. Paul insists that "the righteousness of God" has been revealed. This verse is clearly connected to the previous one by the word *gar*, translated as "for." What is this "righteousness of God"? In the first place it likely refers to God's moral character, which has been revealed in the Scriptures and more clearly in the death of Jesus for all sin. This word *righteousness* and its cognates—righteous, to make righteous, to set right, justice, to be just, and so on—will be the constant theme throughout the following discourse. The righteousness of God, however, refers not only to his justice (an example of which we see in Romans 1:18–32), but to his work of redemption as well. God is not merely interested in meting out justice in a wicked and sinful world, but he is also interested in redeeming that world. And so paradoxically we can talk about God's redemptive judgments. He chastens those he loves, and any judgments prior to the final judgment are meant to be disciplinary, not punitive.

The next phrase literally reads in the Greek "from faith" or "the faithful one unto faith." This is the phrase that Martin Luther surprisingly and wrongly translated "by faith alone." More likely Paul means "from the faithful One (either God or Jesus) unto those who have faith." This makes verses 16–17 more nearly parallel, both referring to the benefits that come from the gospel for those who have faith in it. This reading makes better sense, too, of another controversial phrase to be found and discussed later in Romans: "the faith of Jesus Christ," which turns out to likely mean "the faithfulness of Jesus" (even unto death on the cross). That's what the obedience of faith meant for Jesus.

But then finally, Paul offers a somewhat edited proof text from the Old Testament, which in this case comes from Habakkuk 2:4. As we have the quotation here the Greek reads "just as it is written 'but the righteous from faith (or faithfulness) shall live'" (author's translation). There are several possible ways to interpret this: (1) but those who are righteous by faith shall live; (2) but those who are righteous shall live by faith; (3) but those who are righteous shall live from faithfulness; (4) but the righteous one shall live from (his) faithfulness. This last interpretation would be the one closest to the Hebrew text of Habbakkuk 2:4, which simply says, "but the righteous person shall live by his faithfulness" (author's translation). One possible reason to prefer option number four is because Paul will go on in Romans 4 to tell the story of Abraham who "believed God and it was credited to him as righteousness." That is, both the faith and the righteousness were Abraham's. There was no substituting of someone else's righteousness for Abraham's. Abraham's faith was reckoned as Abraham's righteousness.

In terms of the Greek word order, most scholars think that the phrase "by faith" modifies "the righteous" rather than "shall live," and I would suggest this is probably correct. If the example of Abraham is already in mind then the point would be that one has right standing with God like Abraham by trusting God, as Abraham did. The verb "[shall] live" here then would refer to everlasting life, not physical life without trouble or trauma. In other words, salvation and everlasting life are gifts that come to the believer who trusts in God and in the good news about Jesus Christ. Having established the theme of the following discourse, Paul will then show how this truth plays out for Jews, Greeks, and even "barbarians."

1. What does Paul mean by "the righteousness of God"?

2. Why is "the righteousness of God" such a crucial concept for Paul?

3. Consider this statement: "He chastens those he loves, and any judgments prior to the final judgment are meant to be disciplinary, not punitive." How might this comment shape your understanding of God? Have you ever wondered if God was punishing you? What might be the difference between being punished versus being disciplined in love?

COMMENTARY NOTES

General Comments. One of the real problems in the study of the book of Romans is that the whole book has been examined profusely by Christians through the ages, read and read again. In the modern era very little account has been paid to the rhetoric of Romans until the last two decades or so. The document has, on the one hand, been read as just a Pauline letter (even though it is nothing like most ancient letters except at the margins of the document), and on the other hand, it has been read as if it were some sort of compendium of Pauline theology, ignoring its specificity in addressing unique social and congregational issues in Rome. As it turns out, Romans is both a highly rhetorical document and highly specific in addressing the social situation in the Roman church. Furthermore, the theologizing and ethicizing we find in Romans is done from and into a specific context and with specific purposes. This is not a one-size-fits-all discourse that was intended to be handed to any and every sort of Christian audience and situation. This of course, in itself, makes it a challenge for the modern reader and user of Romans. What happens when we are reading and studying Romans with an audience nothing like Paul's audience in this letter? What happens if our concerns and major interests are not those of the apostle to the Gentiles? Unfortunately, what usually happens in the race to the application finish line is that we misuse

this precious document and misapply its lessons. Hopefully this study will help us to avoid these pitfalls.

Fortunately for us all, there are not a lot of technical text-critical problems in Romans, unlike many other New Testament documents. Only rarely do the variants we find affect interpretation and meaning in any significant or dramatic way. This is especially good news because the actual challenge of the substance of this discourse is so considerable that it is with a sigh of relief that we do not to have to deal with all sorts of viable textual variants that change the whole way we read a passage.

Day 5, verse 17. Here is a good place for a comment about the controversial phrase *dikaiosune theou*, "the righteousness of God." Sometimes this phrase has been taken to refer to God's covenant faithfulness, perhaps especially in light of some of the things Paul says in Romans 9–11. In other words, it is a catchphrase that does not denote what it seems to on the surface of the words. There are problems with this whole approach to the matter. In the first place, the main audience of Romans, as almost all scholars agree, is Gentile. It is not addressed to a largely Jewish Christian audience. As such, it needs to be kept in mind that the God of the Bible had no prior obligations to Gentiles. He had no covenant with them before the new covenant. So it would hardly be apt for Paul to begin addressing the largely Gentile audience in Rome and talk to them about God's wonderful covenant faithfulness which he did not owe to them! Secondly, while Paul will go on to say that God has not forgotten nor forsaken his first chosen people, the Jews, at the same time Paul is well aware and affirms that the Jews have broken the Mosaic covenant, again and again, and especially so in rejecting their own Messiah! When a covenant is broken, God has no longer an obligation to keep it. All covenants were conditional in nature and led to promises like the following one: "if my people, who are called by my name, will humble themselves and pray and seek my face and turn from their wicked ways, then I will hear from heaven, and I will forgive their sin and will heal their land" (2 Chron. 7:14). Notice the condition.

No, Paul is not talking about God's covenant faithfulness in using the phrase "the righteousness of God," he is talking about God being true *to his own character*, his own nature—both just and merciful, but fair and compassionate, both righteous and loving. Furthermore, he is talking about God's intent not merely to judge the world's sin, but also his intent to set right the sinner! It is not an either-or matter. It involves both judgment and redemption, and indeed redemption through judgment on the cross. We can even use the phrase redemptive-judgment to talk about God's dealings with his people, including the Gentiles. God's ultimate aim is the rectifying of the situation in a fallen world, where all are like Adam and have sinned and lack now the glorious presence of God in their lives.

This leads to a further key point. Since Paul is largely addressing Gentiles and talking about them until Romans 9–11, not surprisingly it is not the story of Israel or the Mosaic covenant or Moses that figures largely in the discussion in Romans 1–8. It is rather the story of Adam (see Romans 5:12–21), a more universal story, a story which resulted in the devastations described in Romans 1:18–32. Paul is quite deliberately putting the gospel on more universal footing by comparing and contrasting the first Adam and his race, and the last Adam, who is Christ, and those who are "in him." This is the story one must keep in view in the reading of Romans 1–8.

WEEK ONE

GATHERING DISCUSSION OUTLINE

A. Open session in prayer.

B. View video for this week's readings.

C. What general impressions and thoughts do you have after considering the video and reading and the daily writings on these Scriptures?

D. Discuss questions based on the daily readings.

1. **KEY OBSERVATION:** In Romans, we have a well-travelled, world-weary apostle who nevertheless is eager to get on with evangelizing the rest of the Gentile world in the western part of the empire. Sometimes reading Paul's letter, and sensing his indefatigable spirit, can just make one tired.

   DISCUSSION QUESTION: Where did all that eagerness, earnestness, and energy come from?

2. **KEY OBSERVATION:** After his conversion, Paul knew all too well that zeal without knowledge can be a dangerous and even deadly thing. Whenever Paul speaks about things he regrets about his past, the one thing that keeps coming up is his zealous persecution, prosecution, and even advocacy of the execution of Christians (see Galatians 1:13 and 1 Corinthians 15:9).

   DISCUSSION QUESTION: What do you notice about Paul's zeal after his conversion? To what did his zeal lead after his conversion?

3. **KEY OBSERVATION:** Paul understood that the church was a voluntary society. People were free to join or to leave. There was nothing compelling them to join the new Jesus movement. This being so, persuasion, powerful persuasion, was often needed to correct or direct a congregation in the ways it should believe and behave.

   DISCUSSION QUESTION: What can the church today learn from Paul's example?

4. **KEY OBSERVATION:** Any kind of justice system is an accountability system, and it can be no accident that justice is one of the things on the mind of Paul when he refers to the righteousness of God, and then goes on to tell the tale we hear in Romans 1:18–32.

   DISCUSSION QUESTION: In what way is a justice system an accountability system?

5. **KEY OBSERVATION:** One of the important things to stress from the outset about Romans is that you need to hear the discourse from start to finish before you really try to evaluate it in detail. It is meant to be heard as it was written out, and its effects are intended to be cumulative.

   DISCUSSION QUESTION: If you have not done so, read Paul's entire letter to the Romans in one sitting. What insight have you gained by doing this?

E. What facts and information presented in the commentary portion of the lesson help you understand the weekly Scripture?

F. Close session with prayer.

WEEK TWO

Romans 3:21–4:25

Righteousness through Faith

INTRODUCTION

The arguments Paul mounts from Romans 1:18 through 3:20 were intended to level the playing field and eliminate any possibility of hubris. The long and short of it was to emphasize that "there is no one righteous, not even one," not Jews and also not Gentiles (see Romans 3:10; Psalm 14:3; and Psalm 53:3). All have sinned, and the ground is level at the foot of the cross. No one is owed nor has anyone earned salvation. Having had dialogues with imaginary Gentile and Jewish teachers in Romans 2 and into Romans 3 (using the rhetorical device called the diatribe), Paul now returns to his thesis statement about righteousness (see 1:16–17) and amplifies it in 3:21–31. He also begins to talk more in depth about how exactly sinners could obtain right standing and begin to be made righteous.

Paul then turns in Romans 4 to the task of showing that God had always had this means of salvation in mind. Already long before the time of Jesus the gospel had been pre-preached to Abraham, who then became the example of trusting God, and his trust and faith were reckoned as righteousness. This was most certainly not a "righteousness that is by [keeping] the law" (see Romans 10:5). God, in other words, showed in advance in the paradigmatic case of Abraham that he had intended to set humanity right, and actually make it righteous through the Spirit's sanctifying power all along—by grace through faith.

This, of course, raised the question of what the possible purpose of the Mosaic law had been if it were not to redeem or save God's people. Paul had an answer ready in hand which he would explain at some length over the course of Romans 5 and 6. Long story short, the Law was meant to keep God's people in bounds until the time had fully come to send the Savior. While the Law was holy, just, good, and reflecting the very character of God himself, the effect of the Law on fallen human beings was not life-giving, rather it was death-dealing. As Paul will put it, the Law effectively turned sin into trespass—a willful violation of a known law.

It is interesting to compare and contrast how Paul uses Abraham as a paradigm in Romans 4 and also in Galatians 3. Both texts quote the key verse from Genesis 15:6, and both texts suggest that the faith of Abraham is the kind of faith that God wants and honors. In Galatians, however, there is more explanation about the connection between Abraham and Christians. Paul will say in Galatians that Christ is "the seed" of Abraham, and that Christians, both Jew and Gentile, become the children of Abraham through faith in Christ. In Romans 4, however, Paul has other purposes in mind.

The net effect of the argument in Romans 4, especially after Romans 3:21–31, is to make clear that salvation involves Gentiles being grafted into the line and legacy of Abraham. This point will be made more fully in Romans 11. Showing at length the indebtedness of Gentiles to the grand forefather of Jews once again prepares for the refutation in Romans 11 of the suggestion that God had forsaken his first chosen people for a new one. To the contrary, Paul will say Gentiles are being grafted into the Jewish tree, the taproot of which is Abraham.

ONE

The Faithfulness of Jesus

Romans 3:21–26 *But now apart from the law the righteousness of God has been made known, to which the Law and the Prophets testify.* [22]*This righteousness is given through [the faith(fullness) of] Jesus Christ to all who believe. There is no difference between Jew and Gentile,* [23]*for all have sinned and fall short of the glory of God,* [24]*and all are justified freely by his grace through the redemption that came by Christ Jesus.* [25]*God presented Christ as a sacrifice of atonement, through the shedding of his blood—to be received by faith. He did this to demonstrate his righteousness, because in his forbearance he had left the* *sins committed beforehand unpunished—²⁶he did it to demonstrate his righteousness at the present time, so as to be just and the one who justifies those who have faith in Jesus.*

Understanding the Word. While Paul is the first to admit that the righteousness of God is borne witness to, in, and by the Mosaic law and the Old Testament prophets, he now wishes to stress that the same righteousness of God has also been given, not merely borne witness to, through faith in Jesus Christ. This phrase—"through faith in Jesus Christ"—may also be translated as the "faith of Jesus Christ" as the King James Version reads. Here we have a technical phrase (see Commentary Notes), which is one of the most controverted of all Pauline phrases in recent discussion. Here it must suffice to say that the phrase probably does not refer to faith in Christ but rather the faithfulness of Christ in light of the following discussion about the atoning death of Jesus. When Paul thinks of Christ's faithfulness, or even his obedience to God's will, he thinks in particular about Christ willingly and freely going to the cross, as in Philippians 2:8 where Paul speaks of Jesus "[becoming] obedient to death—even death on a cross!" Notice how at the end of verse 22 we are told that "this righteousness" is given to "all who believe." Reading the sentence as "this righteousness is given through faith in Christ to those who believe," involves a redundant reference to faith in Christ in two consecutive phrases. This seems unlikely.

Verse 22b makes an astounding point—"there is no difference between Jew and Gentile"! Well, of course, there are many differences between Jews and Gentiles, however, Paul means that they are both on the same footing with God because "all have sinned." It is possible to translate the second half of verse 23 as "and fall short of the glory of God," as if the glory of God was some sort of goal that humans should strive for. This, however, is probably not Paul's meaning. Usually, "glory of God" refers to the living presence of God, or the bright and shining manifestation of God's presence, as once shone on the face of Moses when he came down from Mt. Sinai (see 2 Corinthians 3). The verb here more likely means "lack" and thus we translate the whole phrase as "all have sinned and lack the glory (i.e., the living presence) of God." This would be a reference to what happened when Adam sinned, a story that undergirds much of what Paul says throughout Romans 1–8, and surfaces directly in Romans 5:12–21.

What was it that rectified this drastic situation of humans being sinners and bereft of God's gracious presence in their lives? Verse 24 tells us directly that all are set right (another variant of the word *righteous*) freely by God's grace by means of the redemption that came through Christ Jesus. The language of redemption comes from the hideous practice of enslaving persons. A slave could be redeemed out of his servitude if his master was willing. There would be a cost, a religious ritual in a temple, and the slave would become a freedman or freedwoman (which is not exactly the same as someone who was a free man or woman). In other words, Christ's death purchased the redemption of all who were slaves to sin.

Lest we think that this death was simply the unilateral act of Jesus, verse 25 tells us that God the Father presented Jesus as the "sacrifice of atonement" or propitiation for our sins (see Commentary Notes). Through the shedding of Christ's blood and through his death—the benefit of which must be received through faith—God paid the price for our sins. Sometimes Christians have mistakenly thought that Paul was talking about paying Satan to let us out of his jail, but this is not at all what Paul has in mind. It is sin that is holding the sinner in bondage, not Satan, and the person to whom the debt for sins is owed is the righteous God himself. So paradoxically, it is God who pays himself the price.

Paul also says that Christ's death was a demonstration "at the present time" of the character of God, in particular his righteousness. A righteous God could not pass over sin forever without dealing with it. For a long time, God had left the previously committed sins unpunished. But as Paul says, God had a way to be both righteous and the one who graciously sets right the sinner—namely, through the atoning death of Jesus. You will notice I have been avoiding the translation "justify" or "justification." The latter is law court language, and while Paul can use forensic language from time to time, even in regard to the matter of salvation, his use of the righteousness language actually has a much broader horizon of meaning. Paul is not interested in talking about sinners being reckoned as righteous by some kind of legal legerdemain. He wants to talk about how the fallen have been stood back upright, and how they even have been made righteous. Not only is their objective standing with God rectified, but also their subjective condition is changed by the atoning death of Jesus. Those in Christ have become new creatures. All this is done on the basis of God's grace, not on the basis of human merit.

1. What do you make of the term "atonement"? Why is it important?

2. Why do you think God passed over sin for so long, but then needed to "demonstrate his righteousness"?

3. The text today teaches that all of humanity are equal before God in our fallen nature. Reflect prayerfully on an area where you have need of being put back upright again.

TWO

The Law of Faith

Romans 3:27–31 RSV *Then what becomes of our boasting? It is excluded. On what principle? On the principle of works? No, but on the principle of faith. ²⁸For we hold that a man is justified by faith apart from works of law. ²⁹Or is God the God of Jews only? Is he not the God of Gentiles also? Yes, of Gentiles also, ³⁰since God is one; and he will justify the circumcised on the ground of their faith and the uncircumcised through their faith. ³¹Do we then overthrow the law by this faith? By no means! On the contrary, we uphold the law.*

Understanding the Word. Paul was not a person who had an allergic reaction to the notions of law, commandments, and obedience to imperatives. Indeed, elsewhere (see 1 Corinthians 9; Galatians 6) he is perfectly happy to talk about the law of Christ. Sometimes Christians have made the mistake of thinking that because Paul says Christians are not under the Mosaic law and covenant that, therefore, grace has replaced law, and thus mere faith has replaced the need for obedience in the process of working out one's salvation. This is not an accurate representation of Paul's views.

In our paragraph for today, Paul first tells us that boasting by either Jews or Gentiles is eliminated when it comes to the matter of salvation and atonement for sin because "all have sinned." God does not owe anyone salvation. Sometimes we make the mistake of saying that it is not fair that this or that group of persons is not saved or has not heard the gospel. Such a statement assumes that salvation is a right, or that it is a justice issue. No, says Paul. It is a mercy issue, not a justice issue. If salvation is by grace through faith, then there are no grounds for boasting. So Paul stresses that a person is set right, or put back into a right relationship with God by faith, quite apart from works of the Mosaic law. You cannot work or worm your way into God's salvation. It is a free gift.

The phrase "works of [the] law" is another argued-over Pauline phrase (see Commentary Notes). Here it must suffice to say that Paul is not just talking about certain works of the Law that were boundary-defining rituals or practices—circumcision, Sabbath-keeping, and food laws, things that set Jews apart from Gentiles. By works of the Law, Paul certainly includes such things, but Paul is actually referring to any and all works of the Mosaic law. As we shall see in Romans 10:4, Christ is both the fulfillment and so the end of the Mosaic law or the old covenant as a way of righteousness. There are, in fact, commandments or imperatives that are a part of the new covenant, but the new covenant is not simply a renewal of the Mosaic one. Indeed, in Galatians 4 Paul will stress that the Mosaic covenant was a temporary and interim covenant, and that the new covenant is linked to and is a fulfillment of the Abrahamic covenant and the promises made to Abraham.

So here, Paul stresses that a person is set right with God quite apart from keeping the Mosaic law, and a key reason for this is that God is the God of both Jews and Gentiles, and he offers salvation to all of them on the same basis—by grace through faith in Jesus. It is not the case that Jews get saved one way and Gentiles another, not true that Jews come into the kingdom by keeping the Mosaic covenant and its law, while Gentiles enter by means of the new covenant and its law. No indeed. Paul believes that there is always only one means of salvation, and always only one people of God at any one time in human history. What is different for Paul now that Christ has come is that the people of God are to be seen as Jew and Gentile united in Christ, or as he puts it in Romans 11, Gentiles grafted into the Jewish olive tree of messianic faith and identity. The Gentiles are the Johnny-come-latelies, the surprising last-minute inclusions of the guest list. So much of what Paul says in Romans is meant to be a humility pill for Gentile Christians in Rome, forcing them to reevaluate their Jewish Christian brothers and sisters and the real basis for their standing in Christ. As Paul will say in Romans 4, their indebtedness to Jews goes all the way back to Father Abraham.

Paul concludes this passage by making clear that while salvation is by faith for both Jew and Gentile alike, just because the Mosaic law isn't a means of salvation doesn't mean law in general has been nullified by faith. To the contrary, says Paul, faith upholds the need for law, commandments, and imperatives. It's not just a matter of trust, but rather "trust and obey, for there's no other way. . . ."

1. In what ways are faith and obedience, or even faith and good works, compatible?

2. In what ways are Jews and Gentiles equal in the sight of God?

3. What does it mean to you today that salvation is a free gift?

THREE
Our Forefather Abraham

Romans 4:1–8 *What then shall we say that Abraham, our forefather according to the flesh, discovered in this matter? ²If, in fact, Abraham was justified by works, he had something to boast about—but not before God. ³What does Scripture say? "Abraham believed God, and it was credited to him as righteousness."*

⁴Now to the one who works, wages are not credited as a gift but as an obligation. ⁵However, to the one who does not work but trusts God who justifies the ungodly, their faith is credited as righteousness. ⁶David says the same thing when he speaks of the blessedness of the one to whom God credits righteousness apart from works: ⁷"Blessed are those whose transgressions are forgiven, whose sins are covered. ⁸Blessed is the one whose sin the Lord will never count against them."

Understanding the Word. It is clear enough by the way Romans 4 begins that Paul intends this passage to be connected directly to what has come before. The question is: "What then shall we say that Abraham, our forefather according to the flesh, discovered in this matter?" The wording of the sentence is odd, especially when the word "our" in this phrase includes Gentiles! Could the point be that since "all have sinned" this would also include Abraham? And thus he is everyone's forefather according to the sinful inclinations, with flesh having a moral sense here? It then becomes clear that even Abraham needed to be set right by God's grace and through faith.

Verses 2–3 state clearly enough that Abraham was set right not by works but rather, with Paul quoting Genesis 15:6 twice (see also Romans 4:22), by faith: "Abram believed the Lord and he credited it to him as righteousness."

Especially in light of the fact that Paul will go on to talk about wages, it is clear that Paul is using here not forensic or legal language but rather business language—the language of credits and debits. This is something Paul the businessman, the tentmaker in Corinth, knew something about.

Notice that there is nothing said in this passage about Christ's faith or righteousness being imputed to Abraham, or to any other believer. To the contrary, it is Abraham's own faith which is credited or reckoned as Abraham's righteousness. Despite the business language, Paul says that this righteousness has nothing to do with works, and nothing to do with God having an obligation to give Abraham right standing because he earned it. Not even Abraham's faith should be seen as a work or something that obligates God to give Abraham righteousness.

In verse 5 we also hear for the first time that God sets right the ungodly. We will also hear later than he sets right the sinner, and even God's own enemies! This sort of argument must have been somewhat shocking to Jews in the audience familiar with how the Psalms keep talking about God vindicating the righteous! No, says Paul, there are none righteous and so God vindicates or sets right the unrighteous, the ungodly, the enemies of God, and yes even Gentile sinners, and without them being obligated to get circumcised and keep the Mosaic law! This sort of message must surely have been part of what got Paul in hot water, indeed even got him stoned, when he preached in synagogues. If you read 2 Corinthians 11:23–33, it becomes clear that Paul was more likely a person who prompted "most wanted" posters being put up in synagogues rather than a person who enjoyed celebrity status as a synagogue preacher.

In the quotation from Psalm 32:1–2 Paul introduces the concept of transgressions being forgiven, of sins being covered, and of sins not being reckoned against the sinner. This whole discussion, however, needs to be seen in the light of what Paul had already said in Romans 3:21–31, where Paul made clear that the basis of God's forgiving of sins was Christ's atoning death on the cross. Forgiveness does not mean that sin was overlooked or not dealt with. It means that Christ's death made it possible for a righteous God to deal with sin without condemning and damning the sinner. Paul has now produced evidence from the Pentateuch in the story of Abraham and from the Psalms for his concept of being set right through faith in God and not through the doing of the works of the Mosaic law.

1. What is it about the Abraham story that you find most compelling?

2. What is the point of quoting Psalm 32 in this passage?

3. Since we are set right through faith in God and not through doing works, what was this faith of Abraham? What does faith look like in your life?

FOUR

Which Came First, Faith or Circumcision?

Romans 4:9–15 *Is this blessedness only for the circumcised, or also for the uncircumcised? We have been saying that Abraham's faith was credited to him as righteousness. [10]Under what circumstances was it credited? Was it after he was circumcised, or before? It was not after, but before! [11]And he received circumcision as a sign, a seal of the righteousness that he had by faith while he was still uncircumcised. So then, he is the father of all who believe but have not been circumcised, in order that righteousness might be credited to them. [12]And he is then also the father of the circumcised who not only are circumcised but who also follow in the footsteps of the faith that our father Abraham had before he was circumcised.*

[13]It was not through the law that Abraham and his offspring received the promise that he would be heir of the world, but through the righteousness that comes by faith. [14]For if those who depend on the law are heirs, faith means nothing and the promise is worthless, [15]because the law brings wrath. And where there is no law there is no transgression.

Understanding the Word. Paul's argument in this subsection of Romans 4 depends heavily on the simple observation that Genesis 15 comes before Genesis 17, and so Abraham had right standing with God before he heard and obeyed God's command to be circumcised. This is a very interesting argument because many early Jews argued their way backward through the Abraham saga, starting with the offering of Isaac as an act of obedience (see Genesis 22) and moving back to Genesis 15 and even Genesis 12. We can see this kind of retrospective arguing in James 2:21 where we hear, "Was not our father Abraham considered righteous for what he did when he offered his son Isaac on the altar?" This rhetorical question leads to the pronouncement that even Abraham was set right or counted as righteous not on the basis of faith alone, but rather on the basis of faith plus what he did (later).

Paul, however, is saying that we must follow the story of Abraham in its chronological (and biblical) order. Abraham was already considered to be righteous just for trusting God and moving on faith. This is an important point for Paul especially because he wants to say that right standing and being considered righteous comes on the same basis for both Jews (who kept the Mosaic law and were circumcised) and Gentiles (who didn't and weren't). Paul then will stress that since circumcision was not a prerequisite for right standing with God, or being considered righteous, circumcision must therefore be seen as a seal of the righteousness Abraham already had by faith. *This,* is how it can be said that Abraham is the forefather of both the circumcised and the uncircumcised—they are both set right or considered righteous on the basis of faith, not on obedience to the Mosaic law.

But in verse 13, Paul will make an additional point: Abraham did not receive the promise of offspring and of being "heir of the world" on the basis of his prior keeping of the law. Here we see another connection between Abraham and Gentiles—Abraham was promised to have even Gentiles as part of his patrimony or inheritance. The heirs of Abraham can't be just those who keep the Mosaic law, not least because Abraham existed before that Law and was counted as righteous before even he was required to be circumcised or to offer his son. The problem with law in a world of lawbreakers and sinners is that instead of producing commendation it produces condemnation of human beings, and indeed it turns sin into trespass—a willful violation of an existing and known law. For Paul trespass or transgression is the worst sort of subcategory of sin. In the Old Testament such sins were called sins with a high hand, or premeditated sins, and for many of them there was no atoning sacrifice that could be offered in Old Testament times (see Acts 13:39). Jesus' death, however, even atoned for sins with a high hand. The Law, says Paul, brings wrath on lawbreakers. This is not the good news, but rather the bad news.

1. If circumcision is the covenant sign of the Mosaic covenant, what is the covenant sign of the new covenant?

2. How can Abraham be the forefather of Gentiles?

3. Today's reading said, "Jesus' death even atoned for sins with a high hand" (premeditated sins). Is there an instance of willful disobedience which you desire to confess to God today?

FIVE

The Father of Many Nations

Romans 4:16–25 *Therefore, the promise comes by faith, so that it may be by grace and may be guaranteed to all Abraham's offspring—not only to those who are of the law but also to those who have the faith of Abraham. He is the father of us all. [17]As it is written: "I have made you a father of many nations." He is our father in the sight of God, in whom he believed—the God who gives life to the dead and calls into being things that were not.*

[18]Against all hope, Abraham in hope believed and so became the father of many nations, just as it had been said to him, "So shall your offspring be." [19]Without weakening in his faith, he faced the fact that his body was as good as dead—since he was about a hundred years old—and that Sarah's womb was also dead. [20]Yet he did not waver through unbelief regarding the promise of God, but was strengthened in his faith and gave glory to God, [21]being fully persuaded that God had power to do what he had promised. [22]This is why "it was credited to him as righteousness." [23]The words "it was credited to him" were written not for him alone, [24]but also for us, to whom God will credit righteousness—for us who believe in him who raised Jesus our Lord from the dead. [25]He was delivered over to death for our sins and was raised to life for our justification.

Understanding the Word. In the case of Abraham, literal fatherhood came late in life; indeed, it came when Abraham and Sarah were well beyond the age at which children were possible. In this passage Paul will take this as an illustration of how God can bring life from the dead. In this case, the dead womb of Sarah. Abraham almost was the father of no one, and when his faith in the promise that he would have children through Sarah faltered, he agreed to have an heir by means of the slave woman, Hagar—a decision which led to a series of unfortunate outcomes. Abraham is both the example of what goes right when you trust God's promises, and what goes wrong when you don't! Paul, however, is focusing on the former and not the latter.

The promise given to Abraham, then, is said to be a promise that comes by faith and grace, and not because of works of the Law. It comes to all of Abraham's offspring, both those who were lawkeepers, and those who simply had the faith of Abraham (i.e., Gentiles). It is because it is on the basis of faith and not the Mosaic law that Abraham can be called "the father of us all," indeed "a father of many nations" in the sight of God. This gives Paul the opportunity in verse 17 to speak of a God who brings life from the dead, and calls into being things that did not exist previously.

Verse 18 is one of those marvelous Pauline passages where Paul coins a memorable phrase: "against all hope, Abraham in hope believed and so became the father of many nations." There comes a point where even the most hopeful of human beings give up hope because there doesn't seem to be any way for the desired hope to be realized. But the God who can create something out of nothing can make a way where, humanly speaking, there is no way. All things are possible for the God of the Bible, even the raising of the dead.

Verse 19 tells us that Abraham, at one hundred, was a dead man walking, his body as good as gone. Similarly Sarah had a dead womb. There was no reasonable hope she could ever bear a child, and of course, in the Old Testament story when God brings the possibility up, Sarah just laughs, from whence comes the name Isaac! It must be said that verse 20 is a bit more positive than the presentation in Genesis on the issue of whether Abraham's faith in the promise faltered or not. Perhaps one could say he continued to trust the promise but became persuaded that it would be fulfilled through his union with Hagar. Paul here, unlike in Galatians 4, does not bring Hagar into the discussion.

Verse 23 tells us something important about Paul's own view of the Scriptures. He says that the phrase "it was credited to him as righteousness," while certain for Abraham, was not written for Abraham alone. It was also written for the much later audience, for "us," both Jews and Gentiles who trusted God, and it was credited to "us" as righteousness. Interestingly, in the case of us, the faith also involves a more particular belief about God than Abraham had—a belief that God "raised Jesus our Lord from the dead"

25

(verse 24), a much more spectacular and important life-giving act than the miraculous impregnation of Sarah.

Verse 25 concludes the discussion with a simple statement of faith: Jesus was delivered by God over to death for our sins, but he was raised to life for our right standing with God as well as our being made righteous. As we have seen abundantly in the first two weeks of this discussion of Romans, Paul is sticking to his main theme or thesis: the righteousness of God and the setting right of the sinner.

1. In what way is God's story like Abraham's story?

2. At the very end of this chapter Paul connects Jesus' resurrection rather than his death with our being set right with God. Why?

3. Is there something in your life, like Abraham's, which seems "against all hope" that you could put believing hope in today?

COMMENTARY NOTES

Day 1, verse 22 and Day 2, verse 28. Among the hot topics in Pauline studies are two phrases we have already encountered—namely, "the faith of Jesus Christ" and "works of the law." A certain reading of these phrases has led to what has been called the New Perspective on Paul, which began with E. P. Sanders' seminal work *Paul and Palestinian Judaism*, and was carried forward by numerous scholars, especially in Britain by J. D. G. Dunn and N. T. Wright. We must deal with each phrase in turn.

The "faith of Christ" or the "faith of Jesus Christ" in the Greek can either be an objective or a subjective genitival phrase. That is, it can refer either to a faith of which Christ is the object or a faith of which he is the subject. In short, it can either mean faith in Christ (so an objective genitive phrase) or the faith/faithfulness of Christ. I have for some time been convinced it refers to the latter. Paul is as concerned with the objective work of Christ on the cross for our salvation, as with the subjective faith and trust we put in that saving work. When Paul wants to refer to faith in Christ he uses a different phrase with a preposition "in" (*eis*) or he uses a participle—"those believing" as we have already seen earlier in Romans. Definitely in favor of the subjective genitive interpretation is the context of the discussion in Romans 3 where we hear all about the atoning death of Jesus.

The second phrase "works of the law" has been argued by New Perspective folk to refer particularly to the boundary markers, rituals, and practices of Jews—circumcision, Sabbath-keeping, and food laws. There are several problems with this whole approach: (1) for Paul, the Mosaic law is a package deal. Indeed, every time he uses the word *nomos* of the Mosaic law, he uses it as a collective noun to refer to the whole thing—all six hundred-plus commandments. This becomes especially clear in Galatians where he warns his new converts that if they get themselves circumcised, it won't be just the boundary laws they will need to keep, but "the whole Law." It's a package deal. When Paul wants to speak of individual laws he uses a different word, the word for commandment (*entole*); (2) had Paul wanted to indicate he was only referring to boundary laws by the phrase "works of the law" he could easily have qualified it with the word "some." This is in fact what we find in 4QMMT, the Qumran text so often cited by New Perspective folks, to indicate Paul didn't mean the whole Law; and (3) the biggest problem with this whole New Perspective way of arguing is that it ignores that Paul sees the Mosaic law as part and parcel of the Mosaic covenant. And in regard to the covenant as a whole, Paul thinks it has been annulled, completed, fulfilled—call it what you will—it is finished and done (see 2 Corinthians 3). If the whole covenant is done, then the Law within the covenant is also done. The new covenant is not viewed by Paul as a continuation or renewal of the Mosaic covenant.

Day 1, verse 25. What was the mercy seat in Old Testament religion? It was the place, on the horns of the altar, where the blood of the lamb was sprinkled in order to produce atonement for sins. Why was it sprinkled there? Because this was the contact point, the horns of the altar where God's presence was thought to be. In other words, it was believed that God's anger against sin did indeed need to be assuaged or propitiated. Paul, I would suggest, also believes this theology from the Old Testament. There can be no forgiveness of sins without first sin being atoned for, hence the need for the perfect sacrifice— the death of Jesus. The ultimate reason for this is the unchanging character of God. As the theme of Romans stresses, God is a righteous God. But God is also a loving God, hence his provision of his Son as a substitute offering for our sins. Jesus is the one person for whom Jesus did not need to die, with the exception of Jesus, the statement "all have sinned" is a very literal statement. Christ's death provided a ransom in the place of our having to provide it (Mark 10:45), which we could not possibly have done. Thus in the death of Jesus we see the full and clearest revelation of the whole unchanging character of God—both just and loving, both righteous and compassionate.

You will notice that there has been no discussion of the idea of "imputed righteousness" in our discussion of Romans 1–4. This is for a good reason— it isn't in there. Despite the popularity of this notion amongst many Protestants since the time of Luther, it isn't a Pauline idea. It is simply not true that when God looks at us, he sees Jesus. God is not deceived about our actual condition at any point in time. It is not true that we are merely cloaked in Christ's righteousness, having no righteousness of our own. To the contrary, we have a righteousness which is (1) credited to us on the basis of our faith, like Abraham, and (2) imparted to us through conversion and the work of the Spirit. Paul certainly says in Philippians 3:9 that he does not have a righteousness of his own (which he had before) that comes from keeping the Mosaic law, but rather a righteousness that comes through the faithfulness of Christ, that comes from God on the basis of faith. Nothing that Paul says there suggests Paul simply means an imputed status where Christ's righteousness counts as ours. Notice the verb "comes" occurs twice. This righteous comes to Paul, enters his very being, on the basis of the death of Jesus. It comes to him from God through Christ. This is not a righteousness that exists only on some heavenly tote board. It is an imparted righteousness. As Paul says so clearly in 2 Corinthians 5:21: "God made him who had no sin to be sin for us, so that in him we might [actually] become the righteousness of God."

Day 3, verse 1. For examples of Abraham's sin, see the story of Hagar found in Genesis 16 and 21, or the story of his passing off his wife as his sister in Egypt in Genesis 20.

Day 4, verse 15. The much-debated Greek term *hilasterion* has been translated all sorts of ways, including mercy seat (a more literal translation), means of atonement, propitiation, and atoning sacrifice. It actually has a rather clear sense in other Greek nonbiblical texts as well as in the Old Testament. The problem is not really with the meaning of the word as much as its theological implications. Some people just don't like the notion that God's wrath has to be assuaged before God can forgive sin.

Day 4. Just as Abraham offered up his only begotten son (by Sarah), Issac, so also God sent forth his only begotten Son to atone for the sins of the world. The story of the binding of Isaac is called in Hebrew "The Akedah" (which means binding). It is interesting that it does not figure more prominently in New Testament theologizing. Here is a poem I once wrote that reflects on the meaning of these stories.

AKEDAH

Did he ponder Isaac
Whilst hanging on the cross
A last-second substitution
Just before all was lost?

Is this why he cried out
"My God, My God" so loud
Showing disappointment
Before a hostile crowd?

Where's God's intervention,
Offering another lamb
Or would He be passed over
A dangling great I AM?

Abandoned but begotten
Left to face his fate?
Would help arrive in the nick of time
Or would it come too late?

"Where's the lamb?" asked Isaac
And told "God will provide"

But Jesus died in plain sight
No place for grace to hide.

Jesus, like old Isaac
An only begotten son,
Isaac was no substitute
But Jesus was the one.

We like sheep have gone astray
Unblemished lambs we're not
God led the One to slaughter
The Passover he'd begot.

Offering isn't finished
Until the sacrifice
For any true atonement
Bloodshed must suffice.

Behold the Lamb of God
Who takes away our sin
God accepts no substitutes
For Jesus, in the end.

WEEK TWO

GATHERING DISCUSSION OUTLINE

A. Open session in prayer.

B. View video for this week's readings.

C. What general impressions and thoughts do you have after considering the video and reading and the daily writings on these Scriptures?

D. Discuss questions based on the daily readings.

 1. **KEY OBSERVATION:** It is interesting that Paul doesn't talk about human beings all being equally created in God's image, and so being of sacred worth.

    DISCUSSION QUESTION: In what way does Paul talk about the issue of human equality? (See my two-volume work, *The Indelible Image*, for more on this.)

 2. **KEY OBSERVATION:** Romans 3:21–31 is an expansion of the thesis statement found in Romans 1:16–17.

    DISCUSSION QUESTION: What is added in the Romans 3 passage?

 3. **KEY OBSERVATION:** Scholars have long debated the question, "Why exactly is death, the shedding of blood in and unto death, necessary for the atonement of sin?"

    DISCUSSION QUESTION: Why do you think this is? What is the most precious gift of all?

4. **KEY OBSERVATION:** The story of Abraham is a compelling one, not merely because it provides a sort of prequel to the story of Christians who are set right and reckoned righteous by grace through faith in God's Son, but also because interestingly, Abraham's story prefigures God's story.

   DISCUSSION QUESTION: In what way does Abraham's story prefigure God's story?

5. **KEY OBSERVATION:** Paul states in 1 Corinthians 15:17: "And if Christ has not been raised, your faith is futile; you are still in your sins." When one really ponders deeply the mysteries of salvation, it becomes clear that the entire story of Christ was crucial for us to be made righteous.

   DISCUSSION QUESTION: What are the other parts of the story of Christ that are crucial for us to be made righteous (i.e., What events took place before and after Christ's resurrection)?

E. What facts and information presented in the commentary portion of the lesson help you understand the weekly Scripture?

F. Close session with prayer.

WEEK THREE

Romans 5:1–21

Reconciled through Christ

INTRODUCTION

Romans 5 is, in fact, not one segment of Paul's argument, but two rather different arguments. Romans 5:1–11 is Paul's first effort at explaining the Christian life as a result of the Christ-event previously described. Up to this juncture, Paul has largely been describing Jews and Gentiles outside of Christ, finishing with Abraham, a Jew who happens to be the paradigm for and prequel to the sort of faith he will predicate of Christians. Along the way, he has also described the means by which we can have right standing with God, and indeed can have our faith credited as righteousness, like Abraham's. In the reiteration of the thesis statement and its amplification in Romans 3:21–31, Paul also explains the objective basis on which this right standing comes—the atoning work of Christ. As it turns out, faith or trust in God is not enough to produce right standing with God. There had to be a divine intervention to make this condition possible.

Romans 5 will focus on the benefits or results of having right standing with God for those in Christ. Then Paul will once again turn to a more broad discussion, using the rhetorical device called *synkrisis*, or comparison. In Romans 5:12–21, Paul will compare and contrast the first Adam and the last or eschatological Adam, namely Christ. It is really not a surprise that in a letter to a largely Gentile audience, Paul's focus is not on the story of Israel, but on the more universal story of Adam and his offspring. This is a story that included Gentiles and Jews alike from the start. (The story of Israel and its offspring will be dealt with in Romans 9–11.) When Paul wants to talk about the intersection of the broader story of humanity in general and the more specific story of God's people, he allows the story of Christ to do the heavy lifting and provide the intersection point. It is through Christ that Gentiles become part of the story of God's people, having always been part of the story of humanity descended from Adam.

Romans 5:12–21 is actually more of a contrast between the first Adam and the last Adam, and it makes clear that Paul believes God began the human race over again with Christ—who is Adam gone right, in contrast to the first Adam. This then sets up the discussion in Romans 6–7 about the fallout from Adam's sin—namely, more sin, more death, and more need for the Law; a story that not only describes Israel's experience, but rather the experience of all those in Adam. This then leads to the final argument for Paul's case in Romans 8, where Christian life in the Spirit is explained in detail, a description that is partially prefigured in the description of Christian life in Romans 5:1–11.

[handwritten: BOTH PAUL AND BEN WITHERINGTON ARE WRONG]

ONE
Peace in Our Time

Romans 5:1–5 *Therefore, since we have been justified through faith, we have peace with God through our Lord Jesus Christ. [2]through whom we have gained access by faith into this grace in which we now stand. And we boast in the hope of the glory of God. [3]Not only so, but we also glory in our sufferings, because we know that suffering produces perseverance; [4]perseverance, character; and character, hope. [5]And hope does not put us to shame, because God's love has been poured out into our hearts through the Holy Spirit, who has been given to us.*

[handwritten: VERB?]

[handwritten: PAUL SAYS WE HAVE TO SUFFER]

Understanding the Word. Paul begins his discussion of the Christian life by saying that first and foremost one of the outcomes or benefits of having obtained right standing with God through faith is that we have peace with God. Paul is prepared to put it this way because he believes that previously humankind was actually at war with God and could even be called God's enemy (see Commentary Notes). Christ is the blessed peacemaker who reconciles us with our righteous God. Put another way, Christ is the all-access pass into the grace in which believers stand and he provides grounds for boasting in the hope of the glory of God. This means full communion with God, not just through a glass darkly, but face-to-face communion with God in the future

[handwritten: NO, PAUL SAYS WE HAVE TO SUFFER]

(see 1 Corinthians 13:12). In the meantime, believers glory in something most ancients would find an odd grounds for boasting or glorying—namely, our sufferings.

Paul speaks of glorying in our suffering not because he had a martyr complex or masochistically enjoyed pain. It is rather because he considered it an honor to suffer for the cause and gospel of Jesus Christ, who died for us. It is also because Paul believes that suffering for Christ produces more Christian character in the sufferer. Like Seneca (the great Stoic philosopher who was the instructor of Nero during his early years as emperor), Paul believes that suffering can be part of God's education of a person, making them a better person. Seneca puts it this way, "Are you surprised if that God, who greatly loves the good, who wishes [us] to become supremely good and virtuous, allots to [us] a fortune that makes [us] struggle?" ("On Providence" 2:5–6).

Romans 5:3–5 then provides us with an excellent example of the rhetorical device of stair-step progression, a progressive chain of logic where one has to supply the verb between the members in the list. Notice that "we know," which introduces the list is the voice of Christian experience, of which Paul had plenty by AD 57. One has to assume or insert the initial verb "produce" to fully make sense of this stair-step argument. The Greek itself simply has "suffering produces perseverance" and then elliptically leaves the verb out so the Greek next says merely "perseverance character, character, hope." Paul is not talking about just any sort of suffering, but rather suffering for the gospel's sake. Perseverance is, by definition, the ability to endure over a considerable period of time, and so to prevail in spite of obstacles. The word for "character" here, *dokime*, actually means "tested character," something that has been put on "trial" (the root meaning of the word) and found good. Notice that Paul stresses that "tested character" produces hope—specifically, eschatological hope.

Hope (*elpida*) in Paul's letters does not refer to just any kind of hope. It doesn't, for example, refer to mere wishful thinking. It is a hope grounded in God's track record of what he has done in the past, and more particularly what he has done in Christ already. The Christian faith has always been intended to be forward-looking in nature. This is why the author of Hebrews says in Hebrews 11:1, "now faith is the assurance of things hoped for, the conviction of things not seen" (NRSV). In both cases, the author is talking about eschatological things God had promised—the return of Christ, the resurrection of the dead, the life everlasting, the new heavens, and the new earth. Paul, likewise, is not talking about just any sort of future and just any sort of hope, but rather a christologically shaped one. Elsewhere he says that if we suffer with and for Christ now, we shall reign in a resurrection body with him later. Too often, Christians have focused too narrowly on either the past and its traditions, thinking that is what Christians should dwell on, or on one's individual narcissistic dreams of a personal utopia in the future. Neither is what Paul puts his hope in and looks forward to.

In part, Paul says what he does because it is already true that some hopes have been realized. He says that already God has poured his love into the believer's heart through the work of the Holy Spirit who has been given to the body of Christ. This is the first reference to the love of God in Romans, and not surprisingly, it will come up again at the climax of Paul's description of the Christian life in Romans 8. There is a promise found there that no outside force or power can separate the believer from God's love in Christ (see 8:35–39). We will also hear about our love for God, a rarity in Paul's letters, when Paul speaks about those "who love God [and] are called according to his purpose" (8:28 NRSV).

1. What sort of peace do you think Paul is talking about at the beginning of this passage?

2. Why does Paul view suffering as potentially a helpful thing for the Christian?

3. Can you reflect upon an area of struggle or suffering in your life that produced more Christian character? Have you ever given thanks to God for this?

TWO

Dying to Meet You

Romans 5:6–11 *You see, at just the right time, when we were still powerless, Christ died for the ungodly. ⁷Very rarely will anyone die for a righteous person, though for a good person someone might possibly dare to die. ⁸But God demonstrates his own love for us in this: While we were still sinners, Christ died for us.*

⁹Since we have now been justified by his blood, how much more shall we be saved from God's wrath through him! ¹⁰For if, while we were God's enemies, we were reconciled to him through the death of his Son, how much more, having been reconciled, shall we be saved through his life! ¹¹Not only is this so, but we also boast in God through our Lord Jesus Christ, through whom we have now received reconciliation.

Understanding the Word. According to Paul, no one has a better sense of timing than God. Thus, for instance, in Galatians 4:4 he talks about "when the set time had fully come, God sent his Son." Or, here in verse 6 we hear that at "just the right time" or "according to the appointed time" Christ died for us (author's translation). Never too soon, never too late. At just the right time. Of course, God's sense of time and timing may be very different from our own. We are all familiar with the biblical saying, "With the Lord one day is as a thousand years, and a thousand years as one day" (2 Peter 3:8 RSV). The Greek term *kairos* means something more than just clock time (for which we have *chronos*). Especially in a context in which it is believed that the eschatological age has already been inaugurated (which Paul does believe), a phrase like "the appointed time" or "the exact right time" means, of course, the propitious moment. This is the sort of thing Brutus in Shakespeare's *Julius Caesar* is referring to when he says:

> There is a tide in the affairs of men,
> Which, taken at the flood, leads on to fortune;
> Omitted, all the voyage of their life
> Is bound in shallows and in miseries. (Act IV, scene 3)

Paul is stressing that God picks the right time to work out his salvation plan, and we need to trust God's sense of timing. Thus he says here that Christ died for us "when we were still powerless." Salvation is not a self-help program. It is a radical rescue of the helpless, the powerless. Such are all persons in the bondage of sin. Notice, as well, it says that Christ died for the ungodly. Not, mind you, for the righteous, or the pious, or the "good people" whoever they might be thought to be, but for the ungodly. This, of course, means both Gentiles and Jews. Paul will go on to say in this passage that

Christ died for sinners and even for God's enemies. What incredible kind of love is this?

As Paul adds, you might expect a really good person to be willing to die for a righteous person or another good person. Thus the tales of how the Maccabees gave their very lives for pious Jews is told in 1–2 Maccabees. But this divine love is a different sort of love, a love of even one's enemies, a love of even the unlovely and ungodly. Who would die for them? The answer is Jesus. I remember Victor Furnish of the Perkins School of Theology at Southern Methodist University once saying that God's love is not like a heat-seeking missile, aimed at something inherently attractive in the target audience. To the contrary, God's love is an "in spite of" love, not a "because of" love. God's love tells us everything about God's character and nothing about ours, except our need. When someone loves you in spite of your previous behavior, and during the very time when you were behaving in a manner that should have disqualified you from receiving such a blessed gift, then you know you are dealing with divine love. This is a holy love, an unconditional love in the sense that it is given without prior conditions or considerations.

Verse 9 reminds us that being set right with God is not all there is to salvation. It is only the first act of the three-part act of salvation—we have been saved, we are being saved, we shall be saved. And one of the things believers are saved from is the future coming wrath or judgment of God on a fallen world. In verse 10, Paul begins to use another term for salvation—"reconciliation." The word implies that the two parties were previously estranged and needed to be reconciled. All the more so when, as Paul says, there was a time when we were God's veritable enemies! God was willing to make peace with his enemies through the blood of the cross, not counting their sins against them. What kind of righteous God is this?

Notice that reconciliation, like initial salvation or right standing, and the beginning of sanctification has already happened for the believer. What is still yet to come Paul calls being "saved through his life," in this case presumably saved from the wrath to come. Reconciliation we already have. Right standing and the beginnings of righteousness we already have. We do not yet have full conformity to the image of Christ by resurrection. It is by resurrection that we shall fully experience everlasting life and dodge the maelstrom that is yet to come.

1. Why is it that we have such a difficult time discerning, and then accepting, God's timing for things?

2. What is it that Paul suggests we should hope for in the future?

3. You just read, "When someone loves you in spite of previous behavior," or even during a time when your actions should disqualify you, ". . . then you know you are dealing with divine love." Can you think back on such a time and give thanks to God today?

THREE

Adam's Rotten Apple

Romans 5:12–14 *Therefore, just as sin entered the world through one man, and death through sin, and in this way death came to all people, because all sinned—*
    ¹³To be sure, sin was in the world before the law was given, but sin is not charged against anyone's account where there is no law. ¹⁴Nevertheless, death reigned from the time of Adam to the time of Moses, even over those who did not sin by breaking a command, as did Adam, who is a pattern of the one to come.

Understanding the Word. A rhetorical comparison often turns out to be more of a contrast than a comparison. It may be useful at this juncture to list first the ways in which the first Adam and the last Adam, Christ, are similar. First, in both cases one man's actions affected a whole group of people. Second, God was starting a whole new race or beginning of humanity with each of these men. Third, to use Pauline terminology, one is either in Adam or in Christ. There is no third category and no neutral territory, and which person one is "in" determines what one inherits. Fourth, Paul states very clearly in verse 14 that Adam is a "type" (*tupos*), or the pattern of the one to come. Just as Abraham is a prefiguration of the Christian in Paul's view, so Adam is a prefiguration of the Christ. We will say more about how typology works in the Commentary Notes. For Paul, however, the dramatic differences between the first Adam and the last Adam certainly outweigh the similarities, as we shall see.

Verse 12 draws something of a conclusion based on 5:9–11. Just as sin entered the world through one man, and death through sin, Paul argues that salvation entered the world through another man, and everlasting life through him (though he fails to complete the comparison or the sentence at this point). It is not clear, however, that Paul is talking about physical death in verse 12. He may mean spiritual death entered the world through Adam. Otherwise, it would be hard to explain why there was a Tree of Life in the garden of Eden alongside the Tree of the Knowledge of Good and Evil. This makes the parallelism with Christ, in fact, clearer, because Paul is not arguing that physical life entered the world through Christ, but rather spiritual or everlasting life, or even resurrection life.

But on the other hand, when Paul says that death comes to all human beings because all have sinned, he may be referring to physical death. At the least, what he is denying in verse 12b is that death came to all people simply through Adam's singular sin. In a sense, Paul is suggesting that each person is their own Adam, though he also believes that fallenness and sinful tendencies affect and infect us all because of Adam.

We are dealing here with a concept of headship. A good analogy would be the concept of federal headship. If the president of the United States declares war on a foreign country, then American citizens are at war with that country, quite apart from our own personal choices. The decision of one person has affected us all. So it was with Adam, and so it is with Christ for those who are in Christ. As Paul will say in 2 Corinthians 5:17, "if any one is in Christ, he is a new creation; the old has passed away" (RSV). This is not because the fallen person had *potential* for change. It is because the change agent, Christ, can truly work miracles and transform a person.

In verse 13, Paul reminds us that sin was in the world before the Mosaic law was given, because of Adam, of course. But sin was not counted as trespass, or a willful violation of a known body of laws, until Moses came along. Verse 14 adds that death reigned from the time of Adam to Moses, even over those who did not sin by breaking a single commandment of God, as did Adam. If this seems unfair, remember that Paul has already told us that all sinned and that "the wages of sin is death" (Rom. 6:23). But sin is a larger category than transgression—a breaking of one of God's commands. There are, for example, sins of omission—things one fails to do that one ought to do. For example, failing to love one's children is a sin of omission.

1. Why is it not unfair that when Adam sneezed, we all caught the cold?

2. What is the connection between sin and death, and what sort of death do you think Paul is referring to?

3. We tend to give much personal attention to sins of commission (those actions we know are wrong and have done anyway). Take a moment and consider and confess any sins of omission (those things you knew were right but failed to do).

FOUR
The Gift Is Not Like the Trespass

Romans 5:15–17 *But the gift is not like the trespass. For if the many died by the trespass of the one man, how much more did God's grace and the gift that came by the grace of the one man, Jesus Christ, overflow to the many!* [16]*Nor can the gift of God be compared with the result of one man's sin: The judgment followed one sin and brought condemnation, but the gift followed many trespasses and brought justification.* [17]*For if, by the trespass of the one man, death reigned through that one man, how much more will those who receive God's abundant provision of grace and of the gift of righteousness reign in life through the one man, Jesus Christ!*

Understanding the Word. As Paul develops his rhetorical comparison, he will use a form of argumentation that takes the form of "if X . . . then how much more Y," coupled with the connection between the "one" and the "many." Salvation is seen clearly enough as a gift. Paul says that if the trespass of Adam (who violated the only negative commandment or prohibition God ever gave him) led to the death of "the many," then how much more did God's grace and the gift that came with it (salvation) by means of the grace of the one man, Jesus, overflow to the many?

Sometimes it is difficult to understand what Paul means by grace. If sin is negative influence, then presumably grace is positive divine influence, which changes things and people. Clearly the term "grace" implies unmerited favor or undeserved benefit, but there is more to it than that. Grace is not some sort of magical substance found in sacraments. It is, as we have said, some kind of divine influence. Notice that grace is connected to a person, not a thing—the grace of the one man Jesus.

In verse 16, Paul states that the gift of God cannot be really compared with the trespass because judgment followed immediately upon Adam's sin. But the gift of God's grace followed after many, many sins and transgressions by millions of people! How much more gracious the gift seems when it comes in spite of a long history of rejecting God's will. The judgment followed Adam's sin, and brought condemnation right away. God, in his forbearance, sent his Son in spite of the fact that human beings, including God's people, kept sinning for generation after generation. And when the gift came, it brought right standing with God, quite unexpectedly. It was a severe mercy that came to humankind through the death of Jesus.

Verse 17 provides a comparison that leads to a contrast. Through the trespass of one man, Adam, death reigned through that one man. But how much more will those who received God's provision of grace, and his gift of righteousness, reign in life through the one man Jesus? Notice that while it is death that reigns in the former case, it is believers through Christ who reign in life, everlasting life, and forever. The effect of Adam's sin is temporal and temporary. The effect of Christ's redeeming grace is both timely and everlasting!

1. How do you view death? What is the difference between spiritual and physical death?

2. In what way is "the gift not like the trespass" if both affected many people?

3. Take a moment and reflect deeply today on this phrase: "Christ's redeeming grace is both timely and everlasting." What thoughts stir in you around this?

FIVE

Where Sin Increased, Grace Increased More

Romans 5:18–21 *Consequently, just as one trespass resulted in condemnation for all people, so also one righteous act resulted in justification and life for all people. ¹⁹For just as through the disobedience of the one man the many were made sinners, so also through the obedience of the one man the many will be made righteous.*

²⁰The law was brought in so that the trespass might increase. But where sin increased, grace increased all the more, ²¹so that, just as sin reigned in death, so also grace might reign through righteousness to bring eternal life through Jesus Christ our Lord.

Understanding the Word. At the conclusion of the rhetorical comparison and contrast between the first and the last Adam, Paul focuses on results. The result of the trespass of Adam, violating exactly one commandment involving a tree, was condemnation for all those who are "in Adam," so, for the whole human race. By contrast, the result of the one righteous act of the last Adam, dying on a cross, a very different tree, was righteousness and life for all people. Of course, that does not happen automatically. It has to be received through faith in Christ. But the more important point is that God's intent and purpose was equally universal to the effects of Adam's sin. God desires that none should perish, but all should have everlasting life. This is plainly implied in Romans 5:18, which means that there is something wrong with an argument regarding Romans 8:28–30 that suggests that God has chosen some to be saved and some to be lost before the foundations of the universe. God's choices reflect and are not in conflict with God's desires and offer of salvation in Christ to all. We will say more about that when we discuss Romans 8.

Notice in verse 19, the clear contrast between being made sinners and being made righteous. Just as Paul would not say that those in Adam are merely reckoned to be sinners, when in actuality they aren't, so he would not say that those in Christ are merely reckoned righteous, though that is true as far as it goes. What the text actually says here is that "through the obedience of the one man [Jesus] many will be made righteous." This agrees with

2 Corinthians 5:21 when Paul refers to our becoming the righteousness of God. This involves not merely our position in relation to God but also our condition. And, furthermore, the contrast here is between the one and the many, not between the many and the all. One man, Adam, is contrasted with everyone else, who are called the many here, and one man, Christ, is likewise contrasted with everyone else. The use of the term "many" here should not be taken to mean "in contrast with all," as if Jesus only died for some, but not all.

The issue of disobedience and obedience is important in Romans, and Paul does not contrast it with faith. Indeed, faith should lead to faithful obedience. And the issue of obedience leads to the discussion of the Mosaic law. Paul is not talking about just any kind of law, say for instance Roman law. Paul says that one of the reasons the Mosaic law was given was to turn sin into trespass, a willful violation of the law of God.

As bad as this may sound, God had an antidote to the effects of the Mosaic law on God's fallen people—namely, give more grace! "So that, just as sin reigned in death, so also grace might reign through righteousness to bring eternal life through Jesus Christ our Lord" (Rom. 5:21). Talk about a gift that keeps on giving!

1. What was the result of the trespass of Adam?

2. What was the result of the one righteous act of Christ?

3. You just read "many will be made righteous," and this is not just changing our position with relation to God, but it is changing our condition. Considering this, as you look back over your life, can you perceive ways you are being made righteous? In what ways are you praying to be made righteous in the coming season?

COMMENTARY NOTES

General Comments. A good deal of the problem for modern interpreters in dealing with a chapter like Romans 5 is that while much of the terminology is familiar, the words have different meanings in our modern context. Take, for example, the word *peace*. When we hear this term, we think of the cessation of hostilities rather than something inherently positive. But, for Paul, while *eirene* (peace) can mean "a cessation of hostilities," the Hebrew word *shalom* has the positive meaning of well-being or wholeness. Hence, Paul is not merely saying that as a result of Jesus' death, God stopped being angry with us. He means God has established a healthy and life-giving relationship with us as well.

Day 1, verse 3. Without question, some Christians have odd ideas about suffering. Some of them, for example, think that if you are a good enough Christian, if you just have enough faith, you don't have to suffer. Sometimes this is called the "health-and-wealth gospel," or even the "faith-promise" notion. Texts like this make clear that such a theology is frankly not biblical. Indeed, Paul will even say that suffering may be a sign that God is working on improving your character. And suffering for Christ is seen as a badge of honor in Paul's view. Even Paul himself says that in his own personal experience, when he was suffering from a stake in his flesh, and he asked God three times to remove it, God's response was no! God said instead that his grace was sufficient to help him endure and prevail over his suffering. Thus, while suffering in itself is not inherently a positive thing, in God's hands, suffering can be used to test and improve Christian character. Indeed, a God who can use the death of his Son to save the world can certainly use our suffering in positive ways.

WEEK THREE

GATHERING DISCUSSION OUTLINE

A. Open session in prayer.

B. View video for this week's readings.

C. What general impressions and thoughts do you have after considering the video and reading and the daily writings on these Scriptures?

D. Discuss questions based on the daily readings.

1. **KEY OBSERVATION:** Spiritual death is a horrible thing. One loses not only the sense of God's presence but even the capacity for a relationship with God. This involves not only the anesthetizing of the conscience so that most any sin can be committed without remorse or sorrow, but it also involves, as Martin Luther said, "the heart turned in upon itself." When Adam sinned he became afraid of God and aware of himself, indeed aware of his naked and vulnerable condition. And so he hid from God.

   DISCUSSION QUESTION: How is Adam's response to his sin characteristic of a person who is estranged from God?

2. **KEY OBSERVATION:** Though often enough we find the Greek phrase translated "eternal life" (verse 21), it would be better if we always translated this phrase "everlasting life" if it is being said of human beings.

   DISCUSSION QUESTION: Why would "everlasting life" be a better translation when referring to human beings and "eternal life" only when referring to God?

3. **KEY OBSERVATION:** In a very real sense, the story told about Adam and Christ in Romans 5 is a story of truth or consequences. We are told that God has set up a moral universe, a universe where actions have consequences, or as Paul puts it in Galatians 6:7, "whatever a man sows, that he will also reap" (RSV).

   DISCUSSION QUESTION: Do you think that Paul means there is an inherent mechanism in life such that bad actions are immediately punished and good ones immediately rewarded, karma theology, or something altogether different? If so, what?

4. **KEY OBSERVATION:** Paul doesn't depict human history like the ancient Greeks where humans are mere pawns of the gods, mere chessmen on the chessboard of rival deities. On the contrary, human actions and human behaviors matter, and indeed can change history.

   DISCUSSION QUESTION: Why does human choice, and freely chosen human trust in God and obedience to God, matter so much to a righteous God?

5. **KEY OBSERVATION:** Sometimes it is difficult to understand what Paul means by grace.

   DISCUSSION QUESTION: Based on this week's study, what do you think Paul means by grace?

E. What facts and information presented in the commentary portion of the lesson help you understand the weekly Scripture?

F. Close session with prayer.

WEEK FOUR

Romans 7:1–25

The Law and Sin

INTRODUCTION

It is fair to say that Romans 7 is the most controverted and controversial chapter in the whole of Romans; in the whole of the Pauline corpus; indeed, in the whole New Testament! No passage has produced more discussion and debate, especially since the time of Augustine, and even more since the time of Luther. At issue are whole theologies about human nature, the normal Christian life, whether people by God's grace can really avoid transgressions, and on and on.

In terms of the flow of the arguments in Romans, Paul has introduced us to Adam and Christ as historical founders and influencers on a whole race of people in Romans 5:12–21. That portion of Romans would be fresh in the minds of the listeners who would hear the material in Romans 7 only a few minutes later, perhaps as little as five minutes later. This is important because when the text suddenly goes from "we" to "I" at 7:7, the audience would have been prepared to ask which of the previously mentioned historical figures might be speaking in chapter 7. They would recognize that Paul was using a very standard and familiar rhetorical device called "speech in character," or, "impersonation." Using this device the speaker would briefly assume the persona of another person, in order to make key points in the argument. In other words, the "I" in Romans 7 is not Paul describing his own experiences, not his experiences before or after his Damascus Road experience, despite what both Augustine and Luther thought. As we shall see, it is Adam who is speaking in Romans 7:7–13, and all those "in Adam" who cry out in Romans 7:14–25: "who will rescue [us] from this body of death" (NRSV). This would not be a surprise to the audience in Rome who relished and appreciated the use of carefully crafted rhetorical devices and arguments.

In fact, Romans 6 develops naturally out of Romans 5:12–21, and leads perfectly into Romans 7. Having introduced the topics of sin, death, and the Law in chapter 5:12–21, Paul will explain the relationship between those three things, and also between salvation, life, and grace as well. In fact, the first two parts of a four-part continuous argument are offered in chapter 6 and this discussion is simply carried to its conclusion in chapter 7. We will focus on the climactic portion of this argument.

ONE
The Law of the Husband

Romans 7:1–4 *Do you not know, brothers and sisters—for I am speaking to those who know the law—that the law has authority over someone only as long as that person lives? ²For example, by law a married woman is bound to her husband as long as he is alive, but if her husband dies, she is released from the law that binds her to him. ³So then, if she has sexual relations with another man while her husband is still alive, she is called an adulteress. But if her husband dies, she is released from that law and is not an adulteress if she marries another man.*

⁴So, my brothers and sisters, you also died to the law through the body of Christ, that you might belong to another, to him who was raised from the dead, in order that we might bear fruit for God.

Understanding the Word. Romans 7:1–4 provides us with an argument by analogy. There are, in fact, two sorts of proofs that a rhetorician might offer—artificial ones and inartificial ones. Inartificial ones are those based on previous custom, law, or sacred text. The kind of argument that one creatively made up out of thin air—a so-called artificial proof—was considered powerful. Paul appeals to his audience's knowledge of preexisting laws about married couples and what happens to the legal situation when one partner (in this case, the husband) dies.

Paul begins by making the rather self-evident point that a wife is bound to her husband until the husband dies, but that when he dies, she is no longer bound to her husband. Among other things, this means that, for Paul, marriage is a temporal institution for our earthly good. Paul does not believe a person remains married in the afterlife, and neither did Jesus, who says that in the resurrection there is neither marrying nor giving in marriage, but rather that we will be like the angels (see Mark 12:25; Matthew 22:30). When the husband dies, the wife is released from "the law that binds her to him." He adds that if she has sexual relations with a man other than her husband while he is alive, then she is rightly called an adulteress. But if her husband dies, she is free to remarry and have sexual relations with her new husband.

At this juncture you may be asking yourself: What has this got to do with Adam and the Mosaic law? Paul explains in verse 4 the point of his analogy: "so [likewise . . .] you also died to the law through the body of Christ, that you might belong to another, to him who was raised from the dead, in order that we might bear fruit for God." That is—believers in Christ are no longer under the Law of the old covenant, they are under the law of the new husband, Christ, and so are under the law of the new covenant—the law of Christ. This, of course, would make especially good sense to Jews previously under the Mosaic law, but Paul had also previously argued in Romans 2 that, to some extent, God's law was written on the hearts of Gentiles as well. Whether Jew or Gentile, neither is under any previous covenant or law, now that one has become the bride of Christ and in-lawed to him.

1. What do you think of Paul's view of the temporal and temporary nature of earthly marriage?

2. In what sense are believers married to Christ?

3. Today's text teaches us that those who are saved/being saved belong to Christ. How does belonging to Christ shape the day that lies before you?

T W O

That Was Then and This Is Now

Romans 7:5–6 *For when we were in the realm of the flesh, the sinful passions aroused by the law were at work in us, so that we bore fruit for death.* *⁶But now,* *by dying to what once bound us, we have been released from the law so that we serve in the new way of the Spirit, and not in the old way of the written code.*

Understanding the Word. In a very real sense, you are never going to understand Romans 7:7–25 unless you see the framework in which it is set— Romans 7:5–6 and Romans 8:1–4. We will concentrate on the first of these two texts here. Suffice it to say that what Paul says in both of these texts is that the Christian person has the Spirit in their lives, and is no longer ruled by the law of sin and death and is no longer in bondage to sin. This being the case, Romans 7:7–25 cannot be about the Christian life, not any genuine Christian life.

In verse 5, Paul tells us that what used to be the case, back then, "when we were in the realm of the flesh" (i.e., ruled by our sinful inclinations), the sinful passions aroused and further stimulated by the prohibitions in the Law bore fruit of a death-dealing kind, not a life-giving kind. Notice the echo of Romans 7:4 where we hear about bearing positive fruit for God. This, says Paul, was the way we were then. Clearly this is a description of life outside Christ.

Then, in verse 6, Paul turns around and tells the audience what is true about both himself and his Christian audience. (Notice the "we" that is used in both verses 5 and 6 which contrasts with the "I" in verses 7 and following.) Paul says that for Christians we have "[died] to what once bound us, and have been released from the law so that we serve in the new way of the Spirit." This will be the last reference to the liberating Holy Spirit until Romans 8:1–4. The person or persons described in Romans 7:7–25 do(es) not have the Holy Spirit in his life, and is trapped in the bondage to sin. Not so for the Christian who has been released from what once bound him or her. Remember that, for Paul, the problem with the Law was its effect on fallen humanity—it turned sin into trespass and made us all even more guilty before God. This is why Paul talks about release from the old written code in verse 6b as opposed to serving in the new way of the Spirit.

In short, the then-and-now contrast in verses 5 and 6 is between what a person once was before he or she became a Christian, and what a Christian now is. This contrast is as stark as day and night. It could hardly be more clear that what follows in the rest of this chapter is not a descriptor of Christian existence.

1. What do you make of the description of life outside Christ in verses 5 and 6, in bondage to one's sinful inclinations?

2. It has been said that when fallen persons think that they can master sin on their own, they, in fact, become slaves to sin and sin becomes the master. Do you agree?

3. Reflect on a time when you attempted to overcome sin on your own. What was the result?

THREE

Adam's Tale

Romans 7:7–13 *What shall we say, then? Is the law sinful? Certainly not! Nevertheless, I would not have known what sin was had it not been for the law. For I would not have known what coveting really was if the law had not said, "You shall not covet." [8]But sin, seizing the opportunity afforded by the commandment, produced in me every kind of coveting. For apart from the law, sin was dead. [9]Once I was alive apart from the law; but when the commandment came, sin sprang to life and I died. [10]I found that the very commandment that was intended to bring life actually brought death. [11]For sin, seizing the opportunity afforded by the commandment, deceived me, and through the commandment put me to death. [12]So then, the law is holy, and the commandment is holy, righteous and good.*

[13]Did that which is good, then, become death to me? By no means! Nevertheless, in order that sin might be recognized as sin, it used what is good to bring about my death, so that through the commandment sin might become utterly sinful.

Understanding the Word. The discourse changes dramatically in verse 7 from what is true about a group called "we" to a story told by "I." But who is this "I" who tells such a sad tale? In the following Commentary Notes, we will talk about how the rhetorical device of impersonation works. Suffice it to say that in its original setting, normally the speaker might even change the sound of his voice, to allow the audience to know that another person was then speaking. The way impersonation worked was that you would first introduce an important historical figure to the audience and then speak as that person—a speech in character, just as we talk today about an actor getting "in character."

In a sense, the impersonation in verses 7–13 is an answer to the rhetorical question, "Is the law sinful?" Paul answers emphatically saying, "Certainly not!" Then the speech in character begins. First the "I" (i.e., Adam) says he would not have known what sin was, were it not for the Law. He then gives an example: "I would not have known what coveting really was if the law had not said, 'You shall not covet.'"

Then, in verse 8, we are introduced to another rhetorical device that will appear more familiar to us: straight personification (see Commentary Notes). Here it is sin that is personified and said to "seize an opportunity." I would suggest we substitute "the snake" for the term "sin" here. So now the verse in question would read: "But [the snake], seizing the opportunity afforded by the commandment, produced in me every kind of coveting. For apart from the law, [the snake] was dead."

Then the speaker gives away his identity clearly—"once I was alive apart from the law." As any good student of the Bible knows, there is only one person who existed before there was any law at all—Adam. Notice, as well, that this speaker keeps talking about "the commandment" as if there were only one. Only Adam had only one commandment to obey (i.e., not to eat of the Tree of Knowledge of Good and Evil. See Genesis 2:17). So he goes on to say, "but when *the* commandment came, [the snake] sprang to life and I died." Here it becomes especially clear that the speaker is talking about spiritual, not physical death. Adam did not instantly physically die once he sinned. He did die spiritually. This is when he became self-conscious, self-focused, and afraid of God because the living presence of God was no longer with him or in him.

Verse 10 is a testimony that the singular commandment Adam was given was intended to bring life, but its violation brought death—spiritual death. Yet another clear clue we are talking about the story of Adam here is the verb "deceive" in verse 11. Adam says the snake took the opportunity to use the commandment to "[deceive] me," a verb elsewhere Paul only uses to talk about that garden story (see 2 Corinthians 11:3 and 1 Timothy 2:14).

After telling this tale, Paul thought it necessary to add for clarity that the real source of the problem was not the Law, indeed the Law was holy, and that single commandment was both righteous and good. A good thing can be used to a bad end, and that is what the snake did in using the commandment to bring about Adam's spiritual death. So we have already in Adam's tale the first example of how sin is made exceedingly sinful, namely, by turning it into transgression.

1. How does the rhetorical device of impersonation make Paul's argument more convincing than it otherwise might have been?

2. What thoughts do you have about substituting "the snake" for the word *sin* in this passage?

3. How does the "I" belonging to Adam shape or change your understanding of this text?

FOUR

The Adamic World

Romans 7:14–20 *We know that the law is spiritual; but I am unspiritual, sold as a slave to sin. [15]I do not understand what I do. For what I want to do I do not do, but what I hate I do. [16]And if I do what I do not want to do, I agree that the law is good. [17]As it is, it is no longer I myself who do it, but it is sin living in me. [18]For I know that good itself does not dwell in me, that is, in my sinful nature. For I have the desire to do what is good, but I cannot carry it out. [19]For I do not do the good I want to do, but the evil I do not want to do—this I keep on doing. [20]Now if I do what I do not want to do, it is no longer I who do it, but it is sin living in me that does it.*

Understanding the Word. The discussion shifts now from past-tense verbs (which we found in verses 7–13 when Paul was describing the past experience of Adam), to present-tense verbs in verses 14–25. Paul is now describing the experience of someone or some group in the present. In light of the whole trajectory of the argument beginning in Romans 1:18–32, which described the fallen world, and continued all the way through 7:7–13, the most logical explanation for what we have here is a description of the current state of those who are in Adam and outside of Christ. In other words, the lost. The only wrinkle we might want to add to that is to suggest that perhaps Paul is dramatically describing a lost person at the brink of salvation, crying out, "Who will deliver me from this body of death . . . this bondage of sin?" This was John Wesley's suggestion, and I think it is a good one.

The discussion begins dramatically with a declaration by the "I" in question. While he recognizes that God's law is spiritual, by contrast this person is unspiritual, and indeed without the Holy Spirit, and so "sold as a slave to sin." Paul is not a believer in the view that all human beings have free will whether they are Christians or not. He believes that non-Christians are in the bondage of sin, whether they realize it or not. They are quite literally not able not to sin, or to put it another way—sin is inevitable in their lives. This person, however, realizes this fact, or at least Paul is describing the condition of this person from his own Christian point of view and depicts him as recognizing his plight.

The "I" here in verse 15 recognizes that his behavior is not logical; indeed, it is puzzling to him. He keeps doing what he hates doing, and what he truly wants to do, he does not do! Illogical! When you think about it, sin truly is illogical. It is self-destructive behavior. At least the speaker is logical enough to recognize that if he does what he ought not to do, and does not ultimately want to do, he is affirming that the Law is an appropriate measuring rod of good conduct.

In verse 17 we have a sort of classic cop-out. The speaker suggests that it must be the case that it's not really him who is driving the train of his life. Rather, it is sin in his life that is making the decisions, and the "I" has abdicated his throne! He says that he realizes that good does not dwell within him, but rather flesh—sinful inclinations. Notice how this matches up perfectly with the description of the non-Christian in Romans 7:5. The desire is there to do good, but there is no will or power to carry it out. The person is an inherent bundle of contradictions. He doesn't do the good he, in his best moments, would like to do. Instead, he keeps making visits to sin city. So again, in verse 20, there is the "devil made me do it" argument, or in this case "my fallen nature made me an offer I couldn't refuse."

1. Do you see the phrase "I couldn't help myself" as a normal complaint of a fallen person, or do you find it as just a form of excuse-making?

2. Do you have sympathy for the plight of the persons described here, or are you just disgusted with them trying to blame the sin in their lives rather than taking responsibility for their misbehavior?

3. Do you agree with Paul that, "non-Christians are in the bondage of sin, whether they realize it or not?" Relate that to your own experience.

FIVE

I Fought the Law and the Law Won

Romans 7:21–25 *So I find this law at work: Although I want to do good, evil is right there with me. *[22]*For in my inner being I delight in God's law; *[23]*but I see another law at work in me, waging war against the law of my mind and making me a prisoner of the law of sin at work within me. *[24]*What a wretched man I am! Who will rescue me from this body that is subject to death? *[25]*Thanks be to God, who delivers me through Jesus Christ our Lord!*

So then, I myself in my mind am a slave to God's law, but in my sinful nature a slave to the law of sin.

Understanding the Word. This last segment of Paul's next-to-last argument before turning to refutations in Romans 9–11 has confused many readers, in part because they did not understand the rhetorical devices in play. For example, more than anything else, what has led some Christians to the view that this must be a Christian speaking is the penultimate exclamation—"Thanks be to God [. . .] through Jesus Christ!" What they did not realize is that this interjection is not the voice of the "I," but rather the interceding of a Christian showing the person the "more excellent way" (1 Cor. 12:31 NRSV). The device is called chain-link construction in which the next argument or speaker is introduced just before concluding the present argument. So, verse 25a is a Christian voice that prepares us for the description of the normal Christian life in Romans 8. It is the reply to the cry of the lost, "Who will rescue me?" Otherwise, everything in Romans 7:21–25b is the voice of the lost person "in Adam" and outside of Christ.

The discussion in verses 21–25 involves the voice of the "I" speaking about two different laws: "the law of [the] mind" and the "law of sin." In both cases it might be better to translate the word *law* as "ruling principle." Paul probably means God's law by the expression "the law of [the] mind" (Romans 2:14–15 describes it even having been written on the hearts of Gentiles by God). The other law referred to here is the ruling sinful inclinations, which dominate the person's actual actions. Paul is perfectly capable of using the term *nomos*, or "law," to mean something other than the Mosaic law. Indeed, in the very next chapter he will contrast the Spirit as a law, or ruling principle, which has set the lost person free from the law of sin and death. Furthermore, it may be best to take Romans 7:21a to mean, "I find this [ruling principle] at work." Paul is not referring either to a law in the Mosaic code or to the law of the Spirit, but the voice is simply saying, "I have found this to be the way things always seem to go. . . ."

The voice of the "I" here says there is a war going on between the law of his mind and the law of the flesh. It's mind-to-flesh combat, so to speak. This person confesses he is a prisoner of his own desires. Sin is the ruling principle that dictates his actions. But at least he knows this is not good. And so in verse 24 we hear the pitiful cry: "What a wretched man I am! Who will rescue me from this body of death?" (NRSV). I would take the latter phrase to mean this fallen body that is heading for physical death, and is already spiritually dead. The good news is—there is an answer!

Verse 25a provides the answer. Thanks be to God it is Jesus who delivers this person. And, interestingly, this deliverer involves both the mind, which is bound to God's law, and the flesh, or sinful inclination, which is bound to the ruling principle of sin. Christ delivers us both from our accuser—the Law—and from our condition—the sinful inclinations.

1. Do you think it is a good thing that this "I" voice here is honest about his condition, but then says he can't do any better on his own?

2. Why have so many interpreters misread this passage?

3. Where do you find yourself living: In patterns of the "I" saying, "Although I want to do good, evil is right there with me," or in the freedom of saying, "Thanks be to God, who delivers me through Jesus Christ our Lord?" What prayers might this inspire you to pray today?

COMMENTARY NOTES

General Comments. The rhetorical device known as impersonation is an important one about which there are extensive rules in the rhetorical handbook, rules which Paul follows very carefully so that his audience in Rome will understand what he is doing. He is assuming the voice of a person other than himself. What Quintilian, the great Roman rhetorician, says about this rhetorical device is that you must first introduce the historical figure you are going to speak as and then you may speak in the first-person as that person, rather than as yourself. Paul clearly does this in chapter 5:12–21 when we hear Adam's story contrasted with that of the last Adam—Christ. The reason for adopting this persona is because Paul cannot describe his own experience in these terms—either when he was an observant Pharisee, or after he became a Christian. To the contrary (see below), Paul says that his Jewish experience and his Christian experience have not really been like this. He was a pious and zealous law-abiding Jew, and now he is a pious and zealous law-abiding Christian.

We must then see the use of this device as a way to describe the plight of fallen human beings—whether Gentiles or Jews, in general. This is what life outside of God and outside of Christ looks like, from a Christian point of view. That last qualifier is important. Romans 7 is not how a Jew nor a Gentile would describe his or her own experience. This is Christian analysis of a pre-Christian condition. Finally, one must account for the change in verb tenses between verses 7–13 and 14–25. The most natural way to do so is to say Paul first talks about Adam's past experience and then about the reality of all those in Adam.

The rhetorical device known as personification is the taking of abstract qualities and giving them personal traits. Sin and grace are personified by Paul on more than one occasion, as are wisdom and righteousness. In Romans 7, it is mainly sin that is personified.

Here it will be useful to offer you the Pauline "I" chart to show you the many and varied ways that Romans 7 has been interpreted down through the years.

Verses 7–13

- the "I" is strictly autobiographical;
- the "I" reflects Paul's view of a typical current Christian experience;
- the "I" reflects the Jewish pre-Christian experience, as Paul viewed it then as a whole;
- the "I" reflects humanity as a whole; or
- the "I" is a way of speaking in general without having a particular group of persons in mind.

Verses 14–25

- the "I" is autobiographical, referring to Paul's current Christian experience;

- the "I" is autobiographical, referring to Paul's pre-Christian experience, as he viewed it then;
- same as previous only it is as he views his Jewish experience now;
- the "I" presents the experience of the non-Christian Jew, as seen by himself;
- the "I" presents how Christians view Jews;
- the "I" reflects the so-called "carnal" Christian;
- the "I" reflects the experience of Christians in general; or
- the "I" reflects a person under conviction of sin, and at the point of conversion (thus Romans 7:14–Romans 8 provide a typical narrative of a conversion).

The thing all of these conjectures have in common (and there have been many more) is that none of them have realized the need to interpret what Paul is doing in light of his use of rhetoric. Sometimes interpreters have noticed the verbal contrast between imperfect-tense verbs in Romans 7:7–13 and present-tense verbs in Romans 7:14–25. The former speaks of someone's past, the latter of someone's present. But often that is as far as it goes.

It cannot be a description of Paul's personal experience in the past because he says quite clearly in Philippians 3:6 that when it came to law-keeping and having a righteousness that could come from the Law, he was blameless. He was not a lawbreaker. This, of course, did not mean he was perfect. Sin is one thing; breaking known laws is another. Paul is simply saying not that he was sinless, but that he was not guilty of being a lawbreaker. The person or persons described in Romans 7:7–25 could never say that. Second, when Paul was a Pharisee he did not view himself as being like the description we find in chapter 7. To the contrary, he says in Galatians 1:14 that he was very zealous for the traditions of his ancestors and was advancing in Judaism beyond his peers! He was no hypocrite, nor is there any evidence he was laboring with a guilty conscience. Apparently, he slept very well at night, and his attitude about the Law was the same as the psalmist in Psalm 119!

John Wesley suggested that 7:14–25 might be the description of a person under conviction of sin, and at the point of conversion. I think this is likely correct. If so, the point here is that Paul has vividly depicted the world, all those in Adam, crying out for redemption.

WEEK FOUR

GATHERING DISCUSSION OUTLINE

A. Open session in prayer.

B. View video for this week's readings.

C. What general impressions and thoughts do you have after considering the video and reading and the daily writings on these Scriptures?

D. Discuss questions based on the daily readings.

1. **KEY OBSERVATION:** One of the things that I often find to be the case about people who live in the Western world is a certain naiveté about human nature. Even remarkably intelligent people can be heard to say things like, "all people are basically good," or the like.

   DISCUSSION QUESTION: What is Paul's view regarding human nature?

2. **KEY OBSERVATION:** The story of the garden of Eden brings into the picture personal evil, by which I mean the figure Christians have come to call Satan. According to the Bible, evil does not just amount to human sin. No, there are also demons and a devil to deal with in the human sphere and in history.

   DISCUSSION QUESTION: Can you think of events in human history that can only be explained by the existence of evil forces in the world?

3. **KEY OBSERVATION:** At some juncture it will be useful to consider how you feel about law, and being a law-abiding person.

DISCUSSION QUESTION: Do you chaff about laws requiring you to keep a certain speed on the highway, or pay your taxes or the like? Are you always a law-abiding person, like Paul seems to have been?

4. **KEY OBSERVATION:** Sin is a huge subject and there are many kinds of sin. The good news for one and all is that Jesus paid it all—for all kinds of sins, once for all time, and we no longer have to be in bondage to sin.

   DISCUSSION QUESTION: What are some different categories of sin?

5. **KEY OBSERVATION:** We often forget that sin is not just an individual matter. It can also be a matter of a pattern of behavior over generations in a family, or even a large group of people. Jesus, however, is a great redeemer, and he can even break this kind of vicious cycle of sin.

   DISCUSSION QUESTION: Have you or anyone you know been affected by generational sin?

E. What facts and information presented in the commentary portion of the lesson help you understand the weekly Scripture?

F. Close session with prayer.

WEEK FIVE

Romans 8:1–17

The Spirit Gives Life

INTRODUCTION

Romans 8 provides us with the climactic argument of the *probatio*, or the arguments *for* the case Paul wants to make with his Roman audience. If you turn the page to Romans 9, you have entered new territory with the beginning of Paul's *refutatio*, his arguments *against* the case that the Gentiles in his audience might make for their superiority over Jews, God's first chosen people. In Romans 8, however, Paul finally talks at length about the Christian life, and it is not an accident that there are some twenty references to the Holy Spirit in this chapter, whereas there were none in Romans 7:7–25. The contrast could hardly be more stark.

Paul has spoken of the character of life in Christ and life in the Spirit briefly before in the amplification of the thesis statement in Romans 3:21–31 and even more directly in chapter 5:1–11, but here Paul pulls out all the stops and provides us with a full glimpse of his views of what the Christian life—vivified, guided, guarded, sanctified by the eschatological Holy Spirit of God—looks like. Here we will learn, among other things, that the Spirit the believer already has in his life is a sort of first installment, or even a down payment of the life to come, which means that the Christian's hope is grounded in what God has already been doing in his or her life. Hope has to do with trusting God to finish what he has begun already. It is not a form of wishful thinking.

ONE

Free at Last, with No Condemnation

Romans 8:1–4 *Therefore, there is now no condemnation for those who are in Christ Jesus, ²because through Christ Jesus the law of the Spirit who gives life has set you free from the law of sin and death. ³For what the law was powerless to do because it was weakened by the flesh, God did by sending his own Son in the likeness of sinful flesh to be a sin offering. And so he condemned sin in the flesh, ⁴in order that the righteous requirement of the law might be fully met in us, who do not live according to the flesh but according to the Spirit.*

Understanding the Word. Romans 8:1 is indeed connected to what has been said in chapter 7 and builds on it. Paul literally says "there is now no condemnation for those who are in Christ Jesus." Obviously the wretched person in chapter 7:14–25 can only hear this as a big relief and good news. But Paul does not tarry on the legal pronouncement of "no condemnation"; he wants to stress that the saved person does not merely have objective right standing with God as a result of Christ's saving work. No, indeed, if anything he is placing the emphasis on the subjective transformation of the person in question.

In fact, you can read the following clause as explaining why there is no condemnation—it is "because through Christ Jesus the [ruling principle] of the Spirit who gives life has set you free from the [ruling principle] of sin and death"! The person in bondage does not receive condemnation, rather he receives liberation, and that is actually why there is no condemnation.

The "law of sin and death" reflects the condition of a fallen world. Sin is just as inevitable as death. And even God's law, the Mosaic law referred to in Romans 8:3, couldn't fix the situation and Paul explains why—"it was weakened by the flesh." I take this to mean that the power and truth of the Law could not in itself overcome human fallenness. Its affect on fallen humanity was not transformative. Indeed, Paul would say it led to condemnation instead of correction. There had to be a more powerful remedy to the human condition than the Law.

Fortunately, says Paul, God did what was necessary by sending his Son "in the likeness of sinful flesh." Paul puts it this way because he does not believe

Jesus was either a sinner or that he bore a fallen human nature. Had he done so, he too would have been in the bondage to sin. Hence the word "likeness" indicates that Jesus did not *appear* any different from any other human being, even though he was dramatically different in his condition, his power, and his abilities. Ironically, the sinless one was sent as a sin offering, to atone for the many sins of humanity. Only when sin was dealt with could a righteous God then pronounce no condemnation and send his transformative Spirit into the life of a fallen person. Notice the verb tense here—the Spirit "has already set you free" (author's translation). This does not mean that one is already perfect or angelic, it simply means one is no longer in the bondage to sin described in Romans 7:14–25. But that, in itself, is reason for celebration. The only remedy for "sin in the flesh" was to condemn sin in the flesh, in the person of the sin-bearer—Jesus.

Verse 4 is crucial to understanding God and the saving ministry of Jesus. The reason God had to do what he did was "in order that the righteous require-ment of the law [in regard to sin] might be fully met in us." We believers live not according to the flesh or sinful inclination, but rather according to, on the basis of, and empowered by God's Holy Spirit. Paul then has explained that the righteous requirements of the Law had to be fully met in us, by their being met for us in Christ himself, who paid the price for our sins.

1. How do you think a person on death row feels when suddenly he is told he has been pardoned by the governor and there is a stay of execution, and indeed in some cases the prisoner is then told he has also been set free (for example because new DNA evidence proved he had not killed someone)?

2. Pardon is one thing, being set free is another. Why are they both so important for it to be possible for anyone to live a Christian life?

3. Are there areas of your life that you feel, "in Christ Jesus," you are being set free from? Take time today to ask Jesus for deeper trans-formation in your life, and in the life of someone who needs this good news.

TWO

Fleshing Out the Flesh Versus the Spirit Contrast

Romans 8:5–8 RSV *For those who live according to the flesh set their minds on the things of the flesh, but those who live according to the Spirit set their minds on the things of the Spirit. ⁶To set the mind on the flesh is death, but to set the mind on the Spirit is life and peace. ⁷For the mind that is set on the flesh is hostile to God; it does not submit to God's law, indeed it cannot; ⁸and those who are in the flesh cannot please God.*

Understanding the Word. What we have in this passage is another rhetorical comparison that is mostly a contrast. In this case, the contrast is not between two persons, but between two forces in a human being's life—flesh, by which is meant sinful inclinations generated by a fallen mortal body, and Spirit, the Spirit of God. As Galatians 5 makes abundantly clear, Paul believes the tension in the Christian is between the sinful inclinations pulling a person in one direction, and the Spirit tugging us in the other direction. The tension is not between the old person and the new person; the old person, as Paul says in Romans 6, is dead and buried if one is in Christ and is a new creation. Paul will unpack in some detail this tension in the Christian life.

Paul says in verse 5 that those who live according to their sinful inclination continue to mentally focus and dwell on those things. But those who live according to the guidance of the Spirit mentally focus on what the Spirit wants in and for our lives. It is interesting to note that God's Spirit has desires for us, plans for us, and hopes for us. This is because the Spirit is a person, not merely a power or a force even though sometimes Christians have thought about and even treated the Spirit in a less than personal way. For example, some people talk like you can get more of the Spirit in your life at some juncture subsequent to conversion, whether it is called "being filled with the Spirit" or something else. The problem with this whole line of thinking is that the Spirit is the third person of the Trinity, not a quantity of power or force. You can no more have "a little bit" of the Spirit in your life than a woman can be "a little bit" pregnant. Either the person of the Spirit is in your life, or he is not. It is, however, true that the Spirit can sanctify more and get hold of more aspects of your personality as time goes on. This is what progressive sanctification means.

While a person may think that they are freeing themselves by freely indulging one sort of sinful inclination or another, Paul says that when the mind is fixated on that sort of stuff, the result is death, beginning with spiritual death. But the mind governed by the Spirit gains both life and peace. So ironically those who try to "live it up" in sin, in fact, are killing themselves, whereas those who focus on the Spirit are gaining more life.

Verse 7 is important because it reminds us of Paul's view of human fallenness. He not only says that the mind that focuses on sinful inclinations is hostile to God and to God's law, such a person doesn't submit to God's law, and *he cannot do so*. Again, this is the person described in Romans 7:14–25, the person outside of Christ and enslaved to sinful inclinations and sinful behavior. Such a person has no capacity to please God.

1. It has been said, "as a person thinks, so he is." Do you agree?

2. Why do you think it is that some people think real freedom is the freedom to sin, or to break God's laws, when Paul says that real freedom is freedom from sin and sinning?

3. In this passage, Paul is stressing that believers need to make a conscious effort to focus on the Spirit and the things of the Spirit. How could you assist the Spirit by focusing on what the Spirit wants for your life? What are you sensing the Spirit is wanting today?

THREE

The Spirit of Life and Death

Romans 8:9–11 *You, however, are not in the realm of the flesh but are in the realm of the Spirit, if indeed the Spirit of God lives in you. And if anyone does not have the Spirit of Christ, they do not belong to Christ. [10]But if Christ is in you, then even though your body is subject to death because of sin, the Spirit gives life because of righteousness. [11]And if the Spirit of him who raised Jesus from the dead is living in you, he who raised Christ from the dead will also give life to your mortal bodies because of his Spirit who lives in you.*

Understanding the Word. Verse 9 is intended as something of a reassurance. It says literally, "You are not in the flesh [sinful inclination] but rather in the Spirit, if the Spirit of God dwells within you" (author's translation). The dominating orientation of the Christian life is determined by the indwelling Holy Spirit. It is interesting that Paul will say both that the Spirit is in the believer and the believer is immersed in the Spirit, like being in an ocean of God's very presence. In such a context, Paul is suggesting a person surely cannot live as if they are dominated by the sinful inclination. The Spirit is too powerful an influence to allow that to happen. This is why elsewhere Paul talks about grieving or even quenching the Spirit in one's life. When a Christian sets out to sin intentionally, the Holy Spirit warns them against it and is grieved when it happens. Paul says that the Spirit lives or dwells in the believer (the verb here is *oikei*). That is, God's living presence has made a home in the life of the believer and has no intentions of leaving or moving unless the person commits apostasy.

Verse 10 says that the Spirit gives life to the believer, even though he lives in a body that is marred by sin and marked for death. But the Spirit doesn't just give life for any reason, rather he gives life to enable godly living, which is to say righteousness, the constant theme of all of Romans.

It is not quite clear in verse 11 whether Paul is suggesting that just as the Spirit literally raised Jesus from the dead (see Romans 1:3–4), so also he will eventually raise believers from the dead (taking the phrase "will also give life to your mortal bodies" literally), or if Paul is drawing an analogy between the resurrection of Jesus and the new life we already now have in the Spirit. In previous verses it was the latter he was referring to, but here he may have the eschatological horizon in view. In any case, the Spirit is the one who gives both spiritual life and physical resurrection life as well. He seems even to think that the Spirit who currently dwells in the believer will continue to do so, and be the agent that eventually raises us from death.

1. Why is the Holy Spirit so crucial to living a Christian life?

2. What does Paul say is the purpose or reason the Spirit gives life to the believer? What sort of life?

3. You just read, "the Spirit is in the believer and the believer is immersed in the Spirit, like being in an ocean of God's very presence." Pray for an awakening of that reality today.

FOUR

Live Free or Die

Romans 8:12–14 *Therefore, brothers and sisters, we have an obligation—but it is not to the flesh, to live according to it.* ¹³*For if you live according to the flesh, you will die; but if by the Spirit you put to death the misdeeds of the body, you will live.*

¹⁴*For those who are led by the Spirit of God are the children of God.*

Understanding the Word. Here Paul actually talks about a believer having an obligation to live a life in, by, and full of the Spirit. When he wants to express more fully the duty he has in mind, he refers to putting to death the misdeeds of the body by means of the aid of the Spirit. Here again, Paul has in mind making a conscious effort to stifle sinful inclinations and, even more important, to kill off bad behavior. Paul doesn't think a believer can manage this on his own, but he does indeed believe that with the empowerment from the Spirit it is doable. Paul seems to envision a relationship between the believer and the Spirit whereby the believer allows himself or herself to be led by the Spirit in the right direction (verse 14). There is this symbiotic relationship between the Spirit giving guidance, empowerment, and leading, and the believer deliberately choosing to reject sin, turn away from paths that lead to misdeeds, and so on.

In other words, just because the Spirit lives in a believer does not mean that the believer will automatically say or do the right thing. The Holy Spirit does not possess the personality of the believer in the way a demon would in demon possession, so that the individual no longer has control over his mind, his will, his emotions, or his behavior. No, the relationship with the Holy Spirit is a personal one, and so the Spirit guards, guides, protects, convicts, enlightens, and empowers. In short, the Spirit acts something like a parent, without simply taking over the life of the child. And as verse 14 makes clear, *child* is the right word. Paul puts it directly, "those who are led by the Spirit are the *children* of God." What characterizes children is their need for outside assistance and help to get through life.

1. What sort of relationship do you have with the Holy Spirit and how do you envision that relationship?

2. Why is the relationship between the Spirit and the believer not like the relationship between a demon and a demon-possessed person?

3. With the Spirit's help, how might you make a conscious effort today to stifle sinful inclinations? Can you name what those inclinations are?

FIVE

We Cry, "Abba, Father"

Romans 8:15–17 *The Spirit you received does not make you slaves, so that you live in fear again; rather, the Spirit you received brought about your adoption to sonship. And by him we cry, "Abba, Father." ¹⁶The Spirit himself testifies with our spirit that we are God's children. ¹⁷Now if we are children, then we are heirs— heirs of God and co-heirs with Christ, if indeed we share in his sufferings in order that we may also share in his glory.*

Understanding the Word. Further to Paul's description of the kind of relationship the believer has with the Spirit, Paul says that while the believer is a child of God, he does not become the Spirit's slave. Unlike a slave, the believer is set free by the Spirit and, furthermore, there is no reason for a Christian to live cowering in fear. Too often Christians succumb to fear-based thinking, which is antithetical to faith-based thinking. Craven fear is definitely not what God inspires in people. He inspires love, and a deep personal relationship with God, our Father. In fact, the Spirit brings about our adoption as sons and daughters of God.

Certainly one of the most interesting passages in Romans 8 is found in verses 15–16. Here, Paul says that once adopted as sons and daughters of God, one has the right to call God, "Abba, Father." The term "Abba" is Aramaic, and it probably is the term Jesus himself used to address God (see Mark 14:36). It is not slang for "daddy," but it is a term of intimacy, one a child would use of his beloved father, something like "father dearest."

Paul also says that it is the Spirit within us that prompts us to cry, or is the means by which we can cry, "Abba, Father." Then we learn that the Spirit testifies on our behalf that we are children of God, as does our own human spirit. If we are legitimate children of God, we then become heirs of God, and indeed, says Paul, co-heirs with Christ, but there is a proviso. We must be prepared to share in Christ's suffering (by which he means suffering for Christ or the gospel, not just any kind of suffering) so that we may also share in Christ's glory when he eventually returns. This last remark reminds us that God has no problem with humans sharing his glory or his Son's glory. Indeed, we shall be conformed fully to the resurrected image of God.

1. What does "Abba" mean? (No points for answering "a Swedish rock band.")

2. Paul does not believe human beings are born children of God, but rather they only become children of God by adoption. Why?

3. Can you identify any fears you are carrying? If fear-based thinking is antithetical to faith-based thinking, take a moment today to call upon Abba, Father, remembering that you are not a slave bound to live in fear.

COMMENTARY NOTES

Day 1, verse 2. There is a textual problem in Romans 8:2. Does the text read "has set you (singular) free" or does it read "has set me free" or does it read "has set us free," or is there no pronoun here at all in the original Greek manuscript? Probably the "me" reading is a correction so that Romans 8:1–2 matches up with the "I" in Romans 7, but the witnesses for this reading are not really that strong. The "you" singular reading is the more difficult reading, and it actually has good attestation both in Western and Eastern (Alexandrian) manuscripts. The point, of course, is that each individual Christian has experienced this liberation by the Spirit or they would not be a Christian at all!

Day 5. Romans 8:14–17 has as a background the process by which a slave became a freed person, and indeed often an adopted son of the former slave owner! The owner of a slave could free the slave, though the slave would have to pay a fee for his manumission. There would be a ceremony in a temple officiated by a priest. What would often follow was an adoption process. When a master was especially fond of a slave and valued his work, he would then adopt the slave as a son or daughter, and so make them an heir of his own estate. Paul is thinking of this whole process when he writes this passage about believers becoming adopted sons and daughters of God. For Paul, of course, only Jesus is God's natural or begotten Son.

Paul does not affirm the Greek notion of the immortal soul. Rather, like Jesus himself (see Luke 23:46), he affirms the notion of the human spirit, which he refers to in this very passage. By the human spirit he means the nonmaterial portion of the human personality that will survive death. It is the spirit that is handed over to God when someone dies. A person who is in Christ survives death as a spirit that goes to be with God, or as Paul puts it in 2 Corinthians 5, to be absent from the body and present with the Lord.

WEEK FIVE

GATHERING DISCUSSION OUTLINE

A. Open session in prayer.

B. View video for this week's readings.

C. What general impressions and thoughts do you have after considering the video and reading and the daily writings on these Scriptures?

D. Discuss questions based on the daily readings.

1. **KEY OBSERVATION:** In the Christian life we have the ongoing tension of living in a fallen mortal body with sinful inclinations pulling us in one direction, and the indwelling Holy Spirit pulling us in another direction. In the middle of this tug of war, we are called upon to crucify the sinful inclinations, or to deliberately keep in line with and in step with the Spirit.

   DISCUSSION QUESTION: How are Christians to do this?

2. **KEY OBSERVATION:** Paul says that though the believer is set free from the law of sin and death, set free from bondage to sin, nonetheless, there is still a tension in the Christian life between sinful inclinations and the leading of the Spirit.

   DISCUSSION QUESTION: How should a Christian deal with this tension?

3. **KEY OBSERVATION:** Sometimes people think that Spirit-directed behavior means the individual loses control or cedes control to another.

   DISCUSSION QUESTION: How does Paul depict the relationship between the Spirit and the child of God?

4. **KEY OBSERVATION:** It is an interesting fact that there is little or no evidence of anyone praying to God as Abba before Jesus did, and after that all sorts of Christians prayed to God as Abba.

   DISCUSSION QUESTION: What does this say about the sense of intimacy with God that not only Jesus had, but then also Jesus' followers had?

5. **KEY OBSERVATION:** In 1 Corinthians 15, Paul talks about Christ's bodily resurrection being the first fruits of the resurrection, with the believer's resurrection at the return of Christ being the latter fruits, so to speak.

   DISCUSSION QUESTION: Can you imagine what a glorious thing it will be to have a body no longer subject to disease, decay, death, suffering, or sin?

E. What facts and information presented in the commentary portion of the lesson help you understand the weekly Scripture?

F. Close session with prayer.

WEEK SIX

Romans 8:18–39

Future Glory

INTRODUCTION

In the second half of Romans 8, Paul is pressing forward to the end of his positive arguments, using some of the most exalted rhetoric in all of the New Testament. Paul will talk about the future, including the resurrection of believers and the renewal of all creation. He will talk about how the Spirit currently aids our prayer life, while we live in hope of the resurrection. Paul reassures the audience that God is in charge of all that is transpiring and that he will work all things together for good for those who love God. It is "those who love [God]" who are said to be destined in advance to be conformed to the image of God's Son, not only in their inward self, but outwardly in the body as well. There is the further reassurance that nothing outside the believer—no person, no force, no thing—can separate us from the love of God in Christ. Paul will go into detail about the things that cannot rip us out of the firm grasp God has on our lives.

All of this is meant to reassure Christians, in an age of uncertainty, suffering, and persecution, that God has not only not abandoned them, he has a glorious future planned for them. Furthermore, this future is tied to the future of the earth, for Paul does not envision the final stage of the afterlife in heaven. To the contrary, he expects it to be rather like it is described in Revelation 20–21, involving a corporate merger of heaven and earth, such that earth takes on the permanent and positive qualities of heaven and is renewed.

ONE

Creation's Liberation

Romans 8:18–21 *I consider that our present sufferings are not worth comparing with the glory that will be revealed in us.* ¹⁹*For the creation waits in eager expectation for the children of God to be revealed.* ²⁰*For the creation was subjected to frustration, not by its own choice, but by the will of the one who subjected it, in hope* ²¹*that the creation itself will be liberated from its bondage to decay and brought into the freedom and glory of the children of God.*

Understanding the Word. It is not just modern scientists who have been telling us that our future is bound up with that of nature. Paul will say in this passage that creatures are not merely dependent on creation for existence, but that the future of creation is bound up with the resurrection future of the creatures. Here we see a view of creation as "subjected to frustration," and the one who subjected it was God. As it turns out, it was not just Adam's descendants that felt the effects of the Fall. It was also all of creation. Perhaps here he has in view the Genesis story of the curse, and how the ground itself was cursed when Adam sinned, which made agriculture difficult.

In verse 18, Paul is not minimalizing or trivializing human suffering. He was in a good position to know exactly how painful and difficult human suffering could be, having experienced plenty of it himself (see 2 Corinthians 11:24–27). Rather, Paul is saying that by comparison the glory that awaits us far outweighs the current suffering. After all, suffering is temporary. There will come an end to it when one dies. Everlasting life, by contrast, is permanent. In 2 Corinthians 4, Paul speaks of the eternal weight of glory that far outweighs our sufferings. He suggests we mentally weigh these two things in the balance and see which is heavier and weightier.

Verse 19 suggests that creation itself is standing on tiptoes, eagerly awaiting the day we get our promotion, the resurrection day when it too will come up for renewal. Creation is waiting for the children of God to be revealed in their new party outfits, and then it too will get dressed for the dance of joy. The creation and its creatures did not choose fallenness, unlike Adam, but rather were subjected with Adam, the one fashioned out of the earth. The freedom and glorious resurrection of believers will also be the signal and trigger for the freedom and restoration of creation. There will be no more bondage to decay, just as the believer has been liberated already from the bondage to sin, and one day will be liberated like creation from the bondage to disease, decay, and death.

Nowhere in this entire discussion does Paul mention heaven. Heaven in Paul's view is an ultra-clean bus station called Paradise, on the way to the resurrection and the new creation of the material universe. The final destiny of Christians is not in heaven, but rather in the kingdom on earth when Christ returns and all things are made new.

1. Do you think it is fair that God subjected creation to fallenness when he subjected and punished Adam and Eve?

2. The word "glory" comes up several times in this passage. What do you think it means?

3. Here Paul says that present suffering cannot be compared with future glory. Reflect today on this reality—your deepest grief, sorrow, loss, pain, and injury by contrast cannot be compared to the goodness that will be revealed.

TWO

The Whole Creation Groans

Romans 8:22–27 RSV *We know that the whole creation has been groaning in travail together until now; ²³and not only the creation, but we ourselves, who have the first fruits of the Spirit, groan inwardly as we wait for adoption as sons, the redemption of our bodies. ²⁴For in this hope we were saved. Now hope that is seen is not hope. For who hopes for what he sees? ²⁵But if we hope for what we do not see, we wait for it with patience.*

²⁶Likewise the Spirit helps us in our weakness; for we do not know how to pray as we ought, but the Spirit himself intercedes for us with sighs too deep for words. ²⁷And he who searches the hearts of men knows what is the mind of the Spirit, because the Spirit intercedes for the saints according to the will of God.

Understanding the Word. There is a lot of talk about groaning in this passage, by which is meant laboring and struggling under the weight of fallenness.

Verse 22 provides an especially clear echo of the story of the Fall in Genesis 2 because it draws an analogy with labor pains. My grandfather once wrote in his Bible that groan means to have a deep desire. I think this gets at some of what Paul is referring to here, particularly when he speaks about the Spirit groaning.

In verse 23 Paul refers to first fruits, and the question to be raised on the basis of the Greek text is: Is Paul referring to the first fruits (of the eschato-logical crop) being the Holy Spirit? This is perfectly possible and so we would translate "the first fruits, that is the Holy Spirit" with one phrase in apposition to the other (author's translation). The other possibility is that Paul means "the first fruits of the Spirit," in which case he is assuming that the latter fruits of the Spirit come later, perhaps at the final resurrection.

In fact, Paul has already suggested in this very chapter that the Spirit is the agent who will raise believers from the dead. What Paul is likely *not* talking about is getting some of the Spirit now, and more of the Spirit later, say through a second blessing experience at which point one becomes a Spirit-filled Christian. The problem with that whole notion is that it treats the Spirit unlike the personal way Paul refers to the Holy Spirit. The Spirit is a person, and you do not have a person as an intimate part of your life by means of an installment plan! Either that person is part of your life, or he is not. So, I take it that even if Paul is referring to the first fruits that come from the Spirit, the latter fruits have to be the future resurrection when we are raised like Christ. In verse 23 as well, Paul suggests that our actual adoption as sons and daughters of God awaits "the redemption of our bodies." In the meantime, we groan in this mortal coil.

Hope, as Paul emphasizes in this passage, is always future-oriented, for who hopes for what they already have? Thus it is true to say of Christians that they live in hope, or at least they ought to do so. In 1 Corinthians 13, Paul says that faith, hope, and love are the three great qualities of the Christian life. No Christian, in Paul's view, should feel or be hopeless. Not ever. As Adoniram Judson, the first Protestant missionary sent from North America to Burma, once said, "the future is as bright as the promises of God." But Paul is not a person who thinks we should stop everything, stand on tiptoe, and expect the return of Christ any moment. Instead, he says we should wait patiently for our resurrection. To this he adds that hope is not something currently seen, by which he means that what we hope for is not yet tangible or visible. Like the author of Hebrews, he believes that "faith is the assurance of things hoped for, the conviction of things not yet seen" (Heb. 11:1 RSV).

In verses 26–27, we hear that the Spirit intercedes for us, because we don't always know how to pray, or at least how to pray rightly. The text seems to suggest the Spirit intercedes through wordless groans, though the old translation "sighs too deep for words" (RSV) is more eloquent. Scholars have debated whether this is a reference to speaking in tongues, which is possible since tongues seems to be an angelic prayer language given as a gift to some believers.

Verse 27 speaks of God who searches our hearts, and knows the mind of the Spirit, as well as our own minds. This being so, one may wonder why we pray, since God knows what we have in mind before we utter a word. It is, of course, because God has chosen to use our prayers to do his will in this world, and it is also because God desires a close relationship with his people, and talking with one another is part of growing closer to one another.

1. What sort of things do you regularly hope and pray for?

2. Is it okay for Christians to groan?

3. Take a few minutes today to talk with God about your hopes. If words are not present, "groan inwardly."

THREE

Do You Know Your Predestination?

Romans 8:28–30 *And we know that in all things God works for the good of those who love him, who have been called according to his purpose. ²⁹For those God foreknew he also predestined to be conformed to the image of his Son, that he might be the firstborn among many brothers and sisters. ³⁰And those he predestined, he also called; those he called, he also justified; those he justified, he also glorified.*

Understanding the Word. Certainly the most-debated verses in all of Romans 8 are these, and here careful attention must be paid not only to what is said, but also what is not said.

Verse 28 is meant to provide assurance to Christians under pressure and perhaps even suffering, that God works everything together for good for those who love him. Notice that this verse does not say everything that happens is good, or even everything that happens is God's will. To the contrary, it says

God is like a weaver, weaving together all sorts of things to a good end. God can even use suffering and sin and even evil for the good of those who love him. Second, we have here the rare phrase "those who love [God]," which in context clearly means Christians—those who have the Spirit of God in their lives and confess Christ. It is then not just anyone who has all things worked together for them. This is a promise for believers.

There are, in fact, two parallel clauses here "those who love [God]" and "[those] who have been called according to his purpose/choice." Both refer to the same group of people. What is less clear is whether there is a reference to God's choice or the human response to God's call. Clearly God is the one who calls here. This could even mean God's call is based on his knowledge of who, by their own choice, will respond to the call. The phrases are elliptical and capable of being explained in several ways, hence the debate over them.

In the Greek, verse 29 is clearly linked backward with the previous verse, so it should be read: "because those whom God foreknew would love him, he destined in advance to be conformed to the image of his Son, so that he might be the firstborn of many brothers and sisters" (author's translation). So just to be ultra clear, this is not about someone being destined to *become* a Christian, but rather it is about the destiny of those who love God, those who have already responded to the call. This is not about being elected to be a Christian, it's about the great and glorious destiny of anyone who is in Christ—namely, that they will be conformed to the image of God's Son at the resurrection, and Jesus will have many kinsmen and kinswomen in the same bodily condition as he is already in.

Verse 30 explains God's role in every step of the process of the salvation of a human being. It says that those who God destined in advance, he also called, and those who he called he set right, and those he set right, he also glorified. Of course, this final sentence of this paragraph refers to both things that have happened and things that have not happened. The point is to make clear that God is involved every step of the way in our salvation. It is not to say that we believers have no role in the process. Of course we do. Paul says this repeatedly elsewhere, but here the stress is rightly on God's almighty power to save, and his great love for his people.

1. What does this text promise to "those who love [God]" and have responded to God's call?

2. Does this text suggest that everything that happens is ultimately God's will, or not?

3. Write down five qualities you have observed in the Scriptures about the life of Jesus, then pray about being conformed in each of those qualities.

FOUR
Let's Go to Trial

Romans 8:31–34 *What, then, shall we say in response to these things? If God is for us, who can be against us?* *[32]He who did not spare his own Son, but gave him up for us all—how will he not also, along with him, graciously give us all things?* *[33]Who will bring any charge against those whom God has chosen? It is God who justifies.* *[34]Who then is the one who condemns? No one. Christ Jesus who died—more than that, who was raised to life—is at the right hand of God and is also interceding for us.*

Understanding the Word. This section, like various other ones in Paul's letters, involves a series of rhetorical questions. The function of such questions is to make what Paul is saying seem obvious to the audience, as if they would naturally agree with the implied assertions. Paul assumes that what he has said thus far in Romans 8, and perhaps especially in verses 28–30, should call for some sort of response from believers—a hallelujah or amen, if nothing else.

The first substantive question is: "If God is for us, who can be against us?" Paul will list all kinds of things that could get in the way of our relationship with God, or separate us from God, but Paul's point is that the biblical God is such a powerful and sovereign deity that there is no valley deep enough or mountain high enough or obstacle large enough to keep God away from his people.

The argument then turns to making a deduction. If God was even prepared to sacrifice his own Son (which he was), why in the world would anyone think that he would withhold the necessary resources for the believer to be conformed to his Son's image? The latter is a lesser gift than the giving of his Son as a sacrifice for the sins of the world. No, if God would give us the life of his Son, why in the world would he withhold all these other good things?

Paul then imagines a scenario where Christians are on trial, and he says, who in the world can bring charges against God's people, when God is the judge, and he is the one who set his people to rights and declared the verdict of no condemnation? Can any mere mortal or angel gainsay that? No, of course not. Furthermore, if we needed a witness for the defense, there is Jesus, the crucified and risen One, sitting in the witness chair at the right hand of the judge, God the Father, and interceding on the believer's behalf. The verdict in this trial is a foregone conclusion.

1. Sometimes you hear people say, "Your God is too small," but what they really mean is, "Your faith is too small in the real God of the universe." Jesus suggested even a mustard-seed-sized faith in the real God should produce results. What do you think?

2. What sort of verdict do you expect to hear when you stand before the judgment seat of Christ and have to give account of the deeds you've done in the body (see 2 Corinthians 5:10)?

3. Take the promise "If God is for us, who can be against us," and repeat it aloud several times slowly. Let this truth settle in deeply today.

FIVE

"Ain't No Mountain High Enough"

Romans 8:35–39 *Who shall separate us from the love of Christ? Shall trouble or hardship or persecution or famine or nakedness or danger or sword? ³⁶As it is written:*

"For your sake we face death all day long; we are considered as sheep to be slaughtered."

³⁷No, in all these things we are more than conquerors through him who loved us. ³⁸For I am convinced that neither death nor life, neither angels nor demons, neither the present nor the future, nor any powers, ³⁹neither height nor depth, nor anything else in all creation, will be able to separate us from the love of God that is in Christ Jesus our Lord.

Understanding the Word. Verse 35 begins the denouement of this final positive argument with another rhetorical question: Who or what can "separate us from the love of God that is in Christ Jesus our Lord?" Paul will then provide us with a long list of things that cannot do so, including angels and demons, and trouble and hardship, and persecution and famine and people wielding dangerous weapons. He adds geographical barriers as well, and throws in the kitchen sink at the end by saying, "nor anything else in all creation." Paul means, of course, that none of these listed things nor anything else like them can separate us from the love of Christ. There is, however, one thing deliberately left off the list—yourself.

While Paul will say that no third-party celestial or terrestrial, no third thing, no high or low place can separate us from the love of God in Christ, you yourself, as Paul knew all too well, can do that. Paul is reassuring the audience that regardless of their physical circumstances, or their judicial circumstances, or their geographical circumstances, none of these kinds of things can separate them from the love of Christ. None of them can snatch the believer out of God's strong grasp.

In verse 36, Paul cites Psalm 44:22. In some ways, this is an odd choice because the context of that psalm tells how in the past God had routed the enemies of God's people, but in the present God's people have been put to shame and been beaten again and again. It even ends with a cry for God to wake up and help his people. Paul may have chosen the verses in question because they at least speak to a people who are under duress and have known persecution. If, however, Paul is relating the verse to himself, rather than the audience, then it becomes intelligible that he is suggesting that he himself has faced danger repeatedly for the sake of the Gentile believers.

It should be noticed that in this entire section Paul has returned to the "we" here at the end of the probatio, referring to Paul and the audience. It is "we" who are more than conquerors, through Christ who loved "us." Yet Paul, in verse 38, turns to his own dramatic profession of faith, and what he is utterly convinced of—nothing shall come between him and his God, nothing shall come between believers and their Savior—not even angels or demons, never mind lesser beings and lesser obstacles. The passage thus ends in a triumphal reassurance to the audience that for those who place their trust in Christ all things are well, and all manner of things will be well even if for a season they appear not to be. Even if one loses one's physical life in the process. Even so, the God who raises the dead shall have the last say, and God's yes to life is louder even than death's no.

1. Did you notice that Paul left out "you, yourself" from his list of things or persons who can't separate you from God?

2. Do you think Paul is suggesting that it should be obvious to any Christian on the basis of the character of God as revealed in the death and resurrection of Christ that nothing is too difficult for God when it comes to our salvation?

3. "Who shall separate us from the love of Christ?" Have you ever strayed from the love of Christ? Where are you today?

COMMENTARY NOTES

General Comments. While it is certainly true that the term *ktisis* can be translated either "creation" or "creature," in chapter 8 it seems clear that the appropriate translation is creation, which is said to be groaning along with, suffering along with, human creatures. This passage is surely written with the story of the Fall ever-present in the background, and the story of the renewal of creation at the resurrection peaking up over the horizon.

Day 3, verse 28. There are several ways to translate Romans 8:28: (1) "but we know that for all those loving God, everything works unto the good, for those called according to purpose"; (2) "but we know that for all those loving God, God works everything for good, for those called according to his purpose"; and (3) "but we know that for all those loving God, God works all things for good, for those called according to choice." Any of these translations is, in fact, possible. There is no pronoun "his" before the word *prothesis*, which can be translated either "purpose" or "choice." The early church father John Chrysostom, in fact, discusses the question of whose choice might be referred to here, and concludes it may be that of the one loving God. In other words, the call is from God, the choice to respond from the believer. If, however, we translate the word as "purpose," this favors the notion that we are talking about the purpose of the caller, not the respondent.

WEEK SIX

GATHERING DISCUSSION OUTLINE

A. Open session in prayer.

B. View video for this week's readings.

C. What general impressions and thoughts do you have after considering the video and reading and the daily writings on these Scriptures?

D. Discuss questions based on the daily readings.

> **1.** **KEY OBSERVATION:** Even with a slight familiarity with what ancient persuasion looked like, it would have been evident to anyone in Rome that Paul was a powerful persuader or, as we would put it, a powerful preacher.
>
> **DISCUSSION QUESTION:** In what ways do you think Paul's use of rhetoric influenced his audience?
>
> **2.** **KEY OBSERVATION:** The repeated theme of God's love, and also of our love for God, binds this whole portion of the discourse together, with a special emphasis on God's love for us.
>
> **DISCUSSION QUESTION:** What have you learned about God's love from this portion of our study?
>
> **3.** **KEY OBSERVATION:** In Romans 8, Paul is not dealing with apostasy; he is dealing with circumstances, persons, and things outside the individual in question that might be thought to be able to separate that person from Christ.

DISCUSSION QUESTION: Why do you think Paul did not include "you, yourself" in this list?

4. **KEY OBSERVATION:** It is hard to miss the passion of Paul and his great pastoral concern for the audience in this passage, even though he had never met the majority of them.

   DISCUSSION QUESTION: What does this passage reveal to you about Paul's heart for Christ and his people?

5. **KEY OBSERVATION:** One way to look at Romans 8 is that it is like the climax to the first movement of Beethoven's Ninth Symphony. That movement is spectacular, but it is followed by several other great movements, especially the final choral movement.

   DISCUSSION QUESTION: Have you ever found yourself not getting past this "movement" in your study of Romans? If so, what has kept you from reading on?

E. What facts and information presented in the commentary portion of the lesson help you understand the weekly Scripture?

F. Close session with prayer.

WEEK SEVEN

Romans 9:1–33

Israel's Unbelief

INTRODUCTION

When one turns the page from Romans 8 to Romans 9, one quickly realizes one is in a different world. Remembering that the main audience of Romans is Gentile Christians, Paul has used quotations from the Old Testament sparingly up to the end of chapter 8. But when one turns to chapters 9–11, it is a veritable Scripture-fest with some forty-five quotations, allusions, or echoes to the Old Testament. Romans 9–11 is a continuous argument, not finishing until the end of chapter 11, and again with a sort of doxological ending to indicate that the argument has been concluded. How do we explain the sudden change in the frequency of the use of Scripture in this portion of Romans?

First, the subject matter of Romans 9–11 is Israel, non-Christian Israel, and its future in the plans of God. God even can be said to be on trial in this passage because the question is raised: Has God forsaken his first chosen people? Paul's emphatic answer, as we shall see, is *no*, a thousand times *no*! But how then to explain why already by the late fifties, the majority of Jews who have heard about Jesus have not embraced him? Paul believes that God has revealed the answer to this mystery to him, and he is determined to share it with his audience. Indeed, Paul emphatically states in Romans 11:13 that he is speaking especially to the Gentiles in his audience.

Chapters 9–11 have both the tone and the tenor of a rhetorical refutation. One of the reasons for the differences between what we have in this argument and what has preceded it is that in Romans 1–8 Paul was presenting his positive case for the nature of the gospel, which was for the Jew first and also the Gentile. But now he must turn to refute counterarguments, arguments which might suggest God had replaced his Jewish people with a new Gentile people of God. As we have noted earlier in this study, there are two main sorts of proofs that one can muster up to support one's case—artificial ones created out of one's own logic and imagination, or inartificial ones where one cites previous customs, laws, or sacred texts. The rhetorical handbooks are clear that the latter kind of proof, or demonstrations, are more weighty. And so now we can truly understand why there is such a plethora of quotations, allusions, and echoes of the Old Testament in Romans 9–11, indeed more than in the whole of the first eight chapters combined!

Paul is demonstrating from the Old Testament that it is not the case that God has turned his back on Israel, indeed Paul will argue Israel still has a future, but it is a future that depends on Christ, as we shall see. Paul is not an advocate of two methods of salvation—one for the Jews and one for everyone else. Nor is he an advocate of the idea that there are ever two peoples of God on earth at any one juncture. Rather, he argues the harder case that since the coming of the Jewish Messiah, Jesus, the true people of God are Jew and Gentile united in Christ. This does not mean the church has displaced Israel nor does Paul call the church Israel, for God is not finished with non-Christian Israel yet. What he does believe is that all the promises and prophecies of God are being fulfilled and will be fulfilled in Christ, and in his body of people.

ONE
Israel's Great Heritage

Romans 9:1–5 *I speak the truth in Christ—I am not lying, my conscience confirms it through the Holy Spirit—²I have great sorrow and unceasing anguish in my heart. ³For I could wish that I myself were cursed and cut off from Christ for the sake of my people, those of my own race, ⁴the people of Israel. Theirs is the adoption to sonship; theirs the divine glory, the covenants, the receiving of the law, the temple worship and the promises. ⁵Theirs are the patriarchs, and from them is traced the human ancestry of the Messiah, who is God over all, forever praised! Amen.*

Understanding the Word. It is hard to miss the anguish in Paul's voice at the beginning of Romans 9, which stands in such contrast to the exhilaration and joy we sensed at the end of chapter 8. We are now in a very different ethos and type of argument, a painful one. Paul begins the argument by swearing, telling his audience that he intends to tell the truth, the whole truth, and nothing but the truth about Israel and God's relationship with Israel. Paul says his heartache is unending for his fellow Jews who have not (yet) accepted Christ. Astoundingly, he even says that he would be willing to give up his salvation, willing to be cursed and cut off from the Christ whom he so dearly loves, for the sake of his own "kinsmen according to the flesh," his fellow non-Christian Jews (NASB). It would be difficult to express one's heartbreak and desire more dramatically than this.

Beginning in verse 4, Paul lists the advantages, patrimony, and heritage that Israel has that Gentiles do not. "Theirs is the adoption to sonship; theirs the divine glory, the covenants, the receiving of the [Mosaic] law, the temple worship, and the promises. Theirs are the patriarchs . . ." Even if Paul had stopped the list at this juncture it would have been very impressive indeed. God had blessed Israel with all these advantages that Gentiles did not have at all before the coming of Christ. Notice that Paul speaks of "covenants" plural. This comports with what he says elsewhere in Galatians 4 where he contrasts the Mosaic covenant with both the Abrahamic covenant and the new covenant. He stresses that the new covenant is the terminus of the Mosaic one, which was an interim arrangement, and the fulfillment of the Abrahamic covenant, even arguing that Jesus is "the seed" of Abraham referred to in the Genesis stories about the promise to Abraham. You will notice that in regard to all these advantages Paul states his argument in a way that asserts that they still have all these advantages.

We must bear in mind that Paul is combating not merely Gentile snobbery, especially Roman snobbery about being better than every other race of people. He is combating anti-Semitism no less, especially in the virulent form that suggests God had abandoned the Jews. So, finally, in this list Paul plays his big trump card: "from them is traced the human ancestry of the Messiah, who is God over all, forever praised! Amen." Here Paul makes clear not only the Jewishness of the person who had saved this largely Gentile audience (something he already stated in Romans 1:3, and now can expound more fully), but he indicates that this Messiah is actually divine, is actually one of the personal representations of the only true God!

Having made this sort of dramatic introduction of his discussion of Israel, it would be hard for the audience to deny that Israel had certain advantages over Gentiles of all sorts. For one thing they had the sacred Scriptures, which was not true of any Gentile religion. They had the revealed will of God, and they had a God who was faithful and true and consistent in character in the way he related to his people. The God of the Bible was not some moody deity as likely to blight as to bless his people, unlike the pagan gods.

1. What do you make of Paul's list of perks or advantages that Jews have?

2. This opening paragraph ends with a bang—asserting not only that Jesus is the Jewish Messiah, but that he is God, and there is only one of those! How do you suppose his largely Gentile audience reacted to this opening salvo?

3. As you consider Paul's anguish over his fellow Jews who have not yet accepted Christ, are there two or three individuals you would pray for today in this regard?

TWO

Election and Selection

Romans 9:6–14 RSV *But it is not as though the word of God had failed. For not all who are descended from Israel belong to Israel, ⁷and not all are children of Abraham because they are his descendants; but "Through Isaac shall your descendants be named." ⁸This means that it is not the children of the flesh who are the children of God, but the children of the promise are reckoned as descendants. ⁹For this is what the promise said, "About this time I will return and Sarah shall have a son." ¹⁰And not only so, but also when Rebecca had conceived children by one man, our forefather Isaac, ¹¹though they were not yet born and had done nothing either good or bad, in order that God's purpose of election might continue, not because of works but because of his call, ¹²she was told, "The elder will serve the younger." ¹³As it is written, "Jacob I loved, but Esau I hated."*

¹⁴What shall we say then? Is there injustice on God's part? By no means!

Understanding the Word. The Romans, not surprisingly after the success of creating a huge empire, had come to believe they were destiny's darlings, and even the gods' favorites. Paul, however, had a different vision of reality and of the human future. Here at the outset of this paragraph he insists that God's Word had said that God would not forsake his chosen people, and that God's Word had not failed. He then proceeds to explain some of the mysteries of the concept of God's election. What we need to understand about election from the outset is that it is a corporate concept. God chose a people to be his people. Nothing is said about God choosing individuals to be a part of the people. And you will notice that election apparently does not guarantee salvation, because Paul will go on to talk about selection within the elect!

The real main focus of election in the Old Testament can be seen when we ask the question: Chosen for what? And the answer is not so that a bunch of individuals can have Yahweh as their personal Savior. God's people are chosen to be a light to the nations, to reveal God's character and will to the world. This is why God chose Abraham's whole family in the first place, why God gave the Law to Moses, why God set up David as king, and so on. You can search the Old Testament high and low and you will discover that even when there is talk about salvation it refers to something temporal—being rescued from Pharaoh or some other enemy, saved from disease or death in some way, and so on. Election is corporate in nature, and missional in purpose. And even when one is amongst God's chosen people, one's election doesn't guarantee one's individual salvation. Thus the story of the people God rescued from Egypt ends up with only two people out of the multitude being blessed and allowed to enter the Promised Land—*two*!

Paul thus says in this passage that not all those who are descended from Israel are really Israel or Abraham's children. Race or physical descent does not alone decide any issue. It is the legitimate children, the children through Sarah, the children of promise that are the chosen line. God's designated purposes were fulfilled through Jacob and not Esau.

1. What does the phrase "God's sovereignty" mean to you?

2. What is meant by corporate rather than individual election?

3. Consider this matter of God's people being "chosen to be a light to the nations, to reveal God's character and will to the world." What does this mean for you today?

THREE

Have Mercy!

Romans 9:15–21 RSV *For he says to Moses, "I will have mercy on whom I have mercy, and I will have compassion on whom I have compassion." ¹⁶So it depends not upon man's will or exertion, but upon God's mercy. ¹⁷For the scripture says to Pharaoh, "I have raised you up for the very purpose of showing my power in you, so that my name may be proclaimed in all the earth." ¹⁸So then he has mercy upon whomever he wills, and he hardens the heart of whomever he wills.*

¹⁹You will say to me then, "Why does he still find fault? For who can resist his will?" ²⁰But who are you, a man, to answer back to God? Will what is molded say to its molder, "Why have you made me thus?" ²¹Has the potter no right over the clay, to make out of the same lump one vessel for beauty and another for menial use?

Understanding the Word. In order to understand this passage, one needs to bear in mind that Paul believes that all human beings, Jew and Gentile, are fallen persons ever since Adam. This is very clear from the earlier arguments in Romans beginning with Romans 1:18–32. Therefore, the discussion of election and selection presupposes this fact, and proceeds on the basis that anyone that God chooses to do this, that, or the other, or to make them his people is an act of pure mercy. Justice is when people get what they deserve from a righteous God, and trust me, you don't want that! What we are not being told in this discussion is that God, before the foundation of the world, destined some to be objects of mercy and some to be objects of God's wrath. No, the presupposition is "all have sinned and fall short of the glory of God" (Rom. 3:23), and so if God were going to be merely fair, all would be judged.

Second, the discussion of Pharaoh in verses 16–17 is referring to the role that God had Pharaoh play in the history of God's people. It should be remembered that the Exodus account says repeatedly that Pharaoh hardened his own heart, and then finally it also says God confirmed him in that hard-heartedness. God deals with fallen persons, not in an arbitrary way, but according to his purpose and also with clear foreknowledge of their own hearts. Neither foreknowledge (and God knows in advance how everyone will respond to his overtures and plans) nor election alone determines the human future. But it would be equally amiss to suggest that God is not actively working in history for those who love him, working all things together for good as Romans 8 promised. Finally, Paul draws an analogy, saying God is like a potter and we are like the clay that he molds. Paul says we have no right to argue with the potter in regard to how he made us. Notice that Paul distinguishes between vessels made for special purposes (i.e., the chosen people) and vessels made for common use. Paul is not saying that unless you are one of the elect, you are of no use, and indeed, he will explain that numerous people who were not Jews could and did become part of the elect group.

1. When you think of God's mercy, what first comes to mind?

2. In what sense is God like a potter and in what sense are we like clay?

3. If "justice is when people get what they deserve," consider what great mercy God has shown to you! Take some time today to give thanks and praise to God for this incredible undeserved mercy!

FOUR

Scripture Says . . .

Romans 9:22–29 *What if God, although choosing to show his wrath and make his power known, bore with great patience the objects of his wrath—prepared for destruction?* [23]*What if he did this to make the riches of his glory known to the objects of his mercy, whom he prepared in advance for glory—*[24]*even us, whom he also called, not only from the Jews but also from the Gentiles?* [25]*As he says in Hosea:*

"I will call them 'my people' who are not my people; and I will call her 'my loved one' who is not my loved one," [26]*and, "In the very place where it was said to them, 'You are not my people,' there they will be called 'children of the living God.'"*

[27]*Isaiah cries out concerning Israel: "Though the number of the Israelites be like the sand by the sea, only the remnant will be saved.* [28]*For the Lord will carry out his sentence on earth with speed and finality."*

[29]*It is just as Isaiah said previously: "Unless the Lord Almighty had left us descendants, we would have become like Sodom, we would have been like Gomorrah."*

Understanding the Word. Sometimes Paul will simply make a homiletical use of a particular passage or idea from the Old Testament, but more often than not he quotes a passage and presupposes some knowledge of its larger original context. As a rhetorical tactic, this may well have forced the largely Gentile audience to turn to their Jewish Christian brothers and sisters and ask for some help as to what the importance and meaning was of all these quotations. Just in this small subsection of the argument, there are four different passages cited—Hosea 2:23; Hosea 1:10; Isaiah 10:22–23 from the Greek Old Testament, the Septuagint (LXX); and Isaiah 1:9. One key thing to note is that the second quotation from Hosea is, in fact, a reference to Israel—they are both the "not my people" who also become somebodies. The point is that God's mercy and compassion were necessary even in the case of God's own people if they were to stand and withstand all the outside pressure to become like the nations around them.

As Paul had already said in Romans 8:28–30, God prepared in advance a glorious future for his people. He calls them "objects of [God's] mercy" because, of course, even God's people have sinned and fallen short. Verse 24 is important because Paul speaks of "us" as both Jew and Gentile from whom God has called people to serve him. The purpose of all these strong assertions is to reassure the audience that not only do they stand by grace, but that God is not finished with Israel yet, and can still make a people out of those who are currently not part of the people of God.

1. Why do you think there is so much stress in this passage on what God does and is doing, and so little on the human response?

2. What do you suppose Paul is referring to when he talks about objects of mercy prepared for glory?

3. Consider today the language of adoption in this text. God calling a people who were not his people and turning orphans into children of the living God. You have been invited/are being invited into this adoption! Might you echo in prayer aloud today (slowly and meditatively) the words from Song of Solomon 2:16, "My beloved is mine, and I am his"?

FIVE

The Pursuit of Righteousness

Romans 9:30–33 *What then shall we say? That the Gentiles, who did not pursue righteousness, have obtained it, a righteousness that is by faith;* [31]*but the people of Israel, who pursued the law as the way of righteousness, have not attained their goal.* [32]*Why not? Because they pursued it not by faith but as if it were by works. They stumbled over the stumbling stone.* [33]*As it is written: "See, I lay in Zion a stone that causes people to stumble and a rock that makes them fall, and the one who believes in him will never be put to shame."*

Understanding the Word. Paul heightens the irony of what he says by stressing that Gentiles who had not pursued righteousness, as defined by Scripture, had surprisingly found it through faith; whereas Israel who had pursued the "right" sort of "righteousness" pursued it in the wrong way, through works of the Law, and surprisingly had not obtained it. Paul does not appear to be talking merely about justification, but rather about living a godly life. Jews already had right standing with God, but in the pursuit of maintaining it they pursued it not through faith but by works of the Law.

Paul adds that they did not obtain it because they stumbled over the stumbling stone—a reference to Christ here. He then quotes a conglomerate citation of Isaiah 8:14 with 28:16, which are meant to convey the notion that God is the one who sent and set up the stone of stumbling—Jesus the Messiah. Tragically they *did* stumble over him, even though he was going to be both the foundation stone of God's people going forward, and the keystone in the arch of God's people holding its Gentile and Jewish members together in unity. The passage concludes with a great promise: "the one who believes in [this stone] will never be put to shame," which refers to the final evaluation of all persons at the last judgment.

1. Why do you think it was difficult for many Jews to accept Jesus as their Messiah in his own day?

2. Why has it become even more difficult over the last two thousand years for Jews to do so?

3. Today's text ends with a promise: "The one who believes in him will never be put to shame." What does this mean for you today?

COMMENTARY NOTES

General Comments. There are seven places in the New Testament that refer to Jesus using the term *theos*, or "God," and one of them is found in Romans 9:5. Paul's discussion of theology proper includes the idea that Jesus may appropriately be called God, not merely God's Son, but also God the Son. Here we see the impetus, the push, which led to Trinitarian thinking about God. While we do not have a full-blown exposition of Trinitarian theology in the Bible, what we do find in the New Testament is the raw data that indicates that this is an important, indeed essential, truth about God—the Father is God, who can be distinguished from the Son, who is also a representation of the one God, and finally the Spirit is also God, God's invisible living presence on the move in human history. In 1 Corinthians 8:4–6, Paul explains the beginnings of how this works out with his own modification of the famous profession of faith called the "Shema": "Hear, O Israel: The LORD our God, the LORD is one" (Deut. 6:4) What Paul does is to explain that the term *God* in that profession refers to the Father, while *Lord* refers to Jesus Christ. The "oneness" of God, then, does not refer to God being a single person, but rather that God is a unified but complex being who expresses himself in three persons who all share the same divine nature. Thus, in Philippians 2:5–11, Paul is happy to say about the preexistent Son of God that he was "in very nature God."

A cautionary word is in order that one hears Paul out by reading the entire argument in Romans 9–11 before evaluating any one verse or passage. Were you to read only Romans 9, you might think that God has predetermined everyone's fate long ago, and that no one can become part of God's people without that predestined choice of God. This way of thinking, however, ignores that Paul views election (whether in Israel or in Christ) as a corporate thing, so that individuals can be grafted in or broken off from the elect group, as he will go on to say in chapter 11. Paul is not giving us a discourse on how individuals get saved in these chapters. He is talking about Israel still being the people of God, and will explain how Gentiles got grafted into the people of God.

WEEK SEVEN

GATHERING DISCUSSION OUTLINE

A. Open session in prayer.

B. View video for this week's readings.

C. What general impressions and thoughts do you have after considering the video and reading and the daily writings on these Scriptures?

D. Discuss questions based on the daily readings.

1. **KEY OBSERVATION:** This material in Romans 9–11 has been seen as some of the most confusing and complex in all of Scripture, in part because of the rich and frequent use of the Old Testament. One of the reasons it has been confusing to Christians is, sadly, probably as few Gentile Christians today really know their Old Testament as was the case when Paul wrote this letter!

   DISCUSSION QUESTION: Why do you think many Christians today do not really know their Old Testament?

2. **KEY OBSERVATION:** Paul is speaking dramatically in this passage, and with great emotion, and one must always take that into account in reading a passage.

   DISCUSSION QUESTION: What do you observe in this passage that shows Paul's great emotion?

3. **KEY OBSERVATION:** As I have suggested, Romans 9–11 must be read in light of the affirmation of universal human fallenness, which is the

backstory to talking about God setting apart a people to be a light to the nations.

DISCUSSION QUESTION: If all have sinned, what does God's choosing of anyone, whether Jew or Gentile, tell you about God's character?

4. **KEY OBSERVATION:** God's electing purposes have to do with his efforts to change the direction of human history as it degenerates into degradation and lostness.

   DISCUSSION QUESTION: When God chose Israel as his people, what were they chosen to do?

5. **KEY OBSERVATION:** We see in the book of Romans that Paul is cautioning the Gentile believers about thinking that God had abandoned his chosen people.

   DISCUSSION QUESTION: What does he do to show his audience this is not the case?

E. What facts and information presented in the commentary portion of the lesson help you understand the weekly Scripture?

F. Close session with prayer.

WEEK EIGHT

Romans 10:1–11:36

Salvation for All

INTRODUCTION

In order to understand Romans 10, one has to follow the argument through to the end of Romans 11. While chapter 9 did not stand on its own, it was at least possible to treat it as a somewhat independent subunit of Romans 9–11, but this is not the case with chapters 10–11. Therefore, our plan of action in this week's study is to look at key selected passages from within Romans 10–11, focusing more on Paul's argument than on the Scriptures he quotes to support it.

The argument goes like this: (1) Israel is mostly lost, having not embraced its own Messiah. This is in spite of the fact that they are still the elect and beloved of God! Election apparently didn't save them; (2) they are lost because they did not embrace "the righteousness of God" (10:3), which comes through faith in Jesus. Rather they tried to establish their own righteousness by keeping the Mosaic law; (3) this, then, necessitated that Christ put an end to that Law as a supposed means of righteousness. In him, the Mosaic covenant reaches its fulfillment, culmination, and end. It's done; (4) putting an end to the Mosaic law and covenant made it possible to offer "the righteousness of God" to everyone, Jew and Gentile alike, on the basis of faith; (5) the way salvation happens for Jew or Gentile is not by election (Jews already had that), but rather by the proclamation of the good news, the hearing of it with faith, the believing of the message in one's heart, and the confession that Jesus is the risen Lord; (6) by offering salvation to everyone by grace through faith, did God thereby reject his first chosen people? Certainly not; (7) the proof of this is Jews like Paul who have embraced Christ. There is still a righteous remnant among God's first chosen people; (8) God is still pursuing his process of selection within the election, and as for those who are not yet believing in Jesus, they have been only *temporarily hardened*, or to use another metaphor, *temporarily broken off*, from the people of God. God is not finished with them yet; (9) actually, God used this rejection by the many Jews to turn around and offer salvation to the many Gentiles; (10) in a reversal of some Jewish expectations, the full number of the Gentiles are going to be brought into the people of God first, and then in like manner, by grace through faith, "all Israel will be saved" (11:26); and (11) this last act of the salvation historical drama, however, will not transpire until "the deliverer [(i.e., Jesus) comes] from [heavenly] Zion" and "[turns] godlessness away from Jacob" (11:26). Until the return of Christ, the return of Israel to God's people will not be completed.

ONE

How Then Shall We Be Saved?

Romans 10:1–15 RSV *Brethren, my heart's desire and prayer to God for them is that they may be saved. [2]I bear them witness that they have a zeal for God, but it is not enlightened. [3]For, being ignorant of the righteousness that comes from God, and seeking to establish their own, they did not submit to God's righteousness. [4]For Christ is the end of the law, that every one who has faith may be justified.*

[5]Moses writes that the man who practices the righteousness which is based on the law shall live by it. [6]But the righteousness based on faith says, Do not say in your heart, "Who will ascend into heaven?" (that is, to bring Christ down) [7]or "Who will descend into the abyss?" (that is, to bring Christ up from the dead). [8]But what does it say? The word is near you, on your lips and in your heart (that is, the word of faith which we preach); [9]because, if you confess with your lips that Jesus is Lord and believe in your heart that God raised him from the dead, you will be saved. [10]For man believes with his heart and so is justified, and he confesses with his lips and so is saved. [11]The scripture says, "No one who believes in him will be put to shame." [12]For there is no distinction between Jew and Greek; the same Lord is Lord of all and bestows his riches upon all who call upon him. [13]For, "every one who calls upon the name of the Lord will be saved."

¹⁴But how are men to call upon him in whom they have not believed? And how are they to believe in him of whom they have never heard? And how are they to hear without a preacher? ¹⁵And how can men preach unless they are sent? As it is written, "How beautiful are the feet of those who preach good news!"

Understanding the Word. Paul turns at the beginning of Romans 10 to the question of how an elect people, who had rejected their Messiah, might yet still be saved. The subject is not how they first became the elect, which was God's call and choice, but how they might yet be saved. Once again the subject of the righteousness of God is prominent and the very theme of this whole discourse; indeed, it is so prominent that Paul, with a rhetorical flourish, even personifies it and has it speak for itself! Paul basically says Israel was ignorant—it neither knew nor submitted to the righteousness of God. Rather as fallen but elect persons, they sought to establish a righteousness of their own—unsuccessfully, which is why they still needed to be saved according to Paul. Verse 4 tells us in dramatic fashion that Christ put an end to all of that. He did so by fulfilling the righteous requirements of the Mosaic law, exhausting its curse sanctions and need for atonement for sins. Thus he made the Mosaic covenant and its law obsolete as a way of maintaining or obtaining right standing with God, or actual righteousness before God.

Then in dramatic fashion the righteousness that is by faith tells us how one can be saved. Not by going on a pilgrimage to heaven to bring Christ down, or hades to raise him again from the dead, but simply by hearing the message of the good news, hearing it with faith and embracing it, and so believing in one's heart and confessing the risen Lord with one's lips. By making this the means of salvation, salvation becomes open to Jew and Gentile alike by grace through faith, without preconditions—without submitting to circumcision and the Mosaic covenant and its law. This outcome should not be a surprise since the God of Israel is also Lord of all peoples, and since all have sinned, none have a claim on God when it comes to salvation. The same Lord is Lord of both Jew and Gentile, and he receives them into the people of God on the very same basis. The interim arrangement of having God's people keep the Mosaic covenant is over now that Christ has come and fulfilled its just requirements. At the end of this segment, Paul quotes Isaiah 52:7, which provides a rationale for Paul not only to be a preacher but to come to Rome so he may proclaim this good news even in the very heart of a Gentile empire.

1. What is the difference between God's election and salvation?

2. What does it mean to say that Christ is the "[culmination] end of the law" (10:4)?

3. What is the universal basis for all human beings to be saved? Write down what they must believe, say, or do in order to be saved.

TWO

Did They Stumble so as to Fall Forever?

Romans 11:1–10 RSV *I ask, then, has God rejected his people? By no means! I myself am an Israelite, a descendant of Abraham, a member of the tribe of Benjamin. ²God has not rejected his people whom he foreknew. Do you not know what the scripture says of Eli´jah, how he pleads with God against Israel? ³"Lord, they have killed thy prophets, they have demolished thy altars, and I alone am left, and they seek my life." ⁴But what is God's reply to him? "I have kept for myself seven thousand men who have not bowed the knee to Ba´al." ⁵So too at the present time there is a remnant, chosen by grace. ⁶But if it is by grace, it is no longer on the basis of works; otherwise grace would no longer be grace.*

⁷What then? Israel failed to obtain what it sought. The elect obtained it, but the rest were hardened, ⁸as it is written, "God gave them a spirit of stupor, eyes that should not see and ears that should not hear, down to this very day."

⁹And David says: "Let their table become a snare and a trap, a pitfall and a retribution for them; ¹⁰let their eyes be darkened so that they cannot see, and bend their backs for ever."

Understanding the Word. In chapter 11, Paul will unveil the mystery that explains both why so many Gentiles have now embraced Christ, and why so many Jews have not. Notice first of all that Paul is still proud of his Jewish heritage, being a descendant of Abraham and of the tribe of Benjamin. He is proof positive that God has not simply cast off Israel in order to embrace a different people group. Paul quotes Deuteronomy 29:4 coupled with Isaiah 29:10 to the effect that God has temporarily blinded the eyes of most of Israel; though a remnant, like Paul and Peter and James, have been saved by grace from this blindness, but only because they had all three seen the risen Lord and become convinced of who Jesus really was. In other words, it took a miracle for even these Jews to embrace the risen Christ!

At first blush, this blinding of some and saving of others might seems arbitrary and cruel, but we must note that Paul is denying that those who have stumbled have fallen permanently and can never be saved. Indeed, as we shall see, Paul believes that they will be saved later. So just because they were not elected to be a part of the first grace wave of Jews joining the body of Christ, that is not the end of the story. Further, as Paul says elsewhere, there have been some Jews all along through his preaching in the Diaspora in Greece, Turkey, Cyprus, and elsewhere, who have embraced the faith, for example Timothy and his mother and grandmother. But without question, it was discouraging to Paul that so many Jews rejected Jesus. But once God revealed to Paul that all was not lost, and there was still hope for Israel, Paul carried on.

1. To what degree do we really need to know *how* God is working out his plan of salvation in the world, if at the end of the day, whoever is saved will be saved by grace through faith in Jesus?

2. Why does Paul believe he was saved as part of the initial vanguard of Jews who embraced Christ? For what purpose was he saved?

3. Imagine today what sort of faith and courage it would take for you to go from one place to another and have the vast majority of people reject your message.

THREE

Broken Off and Grafted In

Romans 11:11–16 *Again I ask: Did they stumble so as to fall beyond recovery? Not at all! Rather, because of their transgression, salvation has come to the Gentiles to make Israel envious. [12]But if their transgression means riches for the world, and their loss means riches for the Gentiles, how much greater riches will their full inclusion bring!*

[13]I am talking to you Gentiles. Inasmuch as I am the apostle to the Gentiles, I take pride in my ministry [14]in the hope that I may somehow arouse my own

people to envy and save some of them. ¹⁵For if their rejection brought reconcili-
ation to the world, what will their acceptance be but life from the dead? ¹⁶If the
part of the dough offered as firstfruits is holy, then the whole batch is holy; if the
root is holy, so are the branches.

Understanding the Word. As the argument progresses, Paul manages to
wrestle a blessing for Jews from the fact that many of them have been broken off
from the people of God temporarily! Paul says their fall is not beyond recovery,
or a later rising up. Besides, the influx of many Gentiles into the body of Christ
could make Jews jealous of the blessedness of these folk. Paul thinks that the
salvation of Gentiles may make some Jews long to participate in such salvation.

Verse 12 reveals for the first time fully how Paul views God's plan, namely
that the temporary loss of Israelites from the people of God meant room was
made and a blessing was possible for many Gentiles to come into the fold: "but
[. . .] how much greater riches will their full inclusion bring!" (11:12). Paul is
looking forward to the eschaton, when another miracle will occur for God's
people, as it did at Pentecost.

In verse 13, Paul tells us plain as day that he is the apostle to Gentiles,
and so properly speaking he is addressing Gentiles in this whole discourse,
though he expects the Jewish Christians in the audience to listen in as well.
Verse 15 must be compared to verse 12 and taken very seriously: "if their rejection brought reconciliation to the world, what will their acceptance be but life
from the dead?" Paul hints that it will be at the resurrection that the "acceptance" will transpire. Verse 16 puts it in a different metaphorical context—his
point is that all Israel was set apart by God so that if the root is holy, so are the
branches, or if the first fruits of the dough are holy, so is the whole batch. These
metaphors intend to make clear that God is not finished with the rest of the
batch of Jews, those currently not in the body of Christ!

1. Why do you think it is that Paul waits until Romans 11 to make clear
    he is addressing mainly Gentile Christians in Rome?

2. Why do you think God chose a Jew like Paul to be apostle to the Gentiles?

3. Here Paul says, "Did they stumble so as to fall beyond recovery? Not at
    all!" Is there perhaps someone in your life who you have written off as
    being beyond recovery?

FOUR
Branching Out

Romans 11:17–24 RSV *But if some of the branches were broken off, and you, a wild olive shoot, were grafted in their place to share the richness of the olive tree, [18]do not boast over the branches. If you do boast, remember it is not you that support the root, but the root that supports you. [19]You will say, "Branches were broken off so that I might be grafted in." [20]That is true. They were broken off because of their unbelief, but you stand fast only through faith. So do not become proud, but stand in awe. [21]For if God did not spare the natural branches, neither will he spare you. [22]Note then the kindness and the severity of God: severity toward those who have fallen, but God's kindness to you, provided you continue in his kindness; otherwise you too will be cut off. [23]And even the others, if they do not persist in their unbelief, will be grafted in, for God has the power to graft them in again. [24]For if you have been cut from what is by nature a wild olive tree, and grafted, contrary to nature, into a cultivated olive tree, how much more will these natural branches be grafted back into their own olive tree.*

Understanding the Word. One of the major metaphors used to describe the people of God is that they are like an olive tree, perhaps the most common kind of tree one could find in the Holy Land. Paul will stretch his metaphor to talk about natural and wild olive branches. This is not a lecture on horticulture or tree taxonomy, but on the way God operates with Jews and Gentiles when it comes to the people of God. The "you" in verse 17 is clearly the Gentile Christians Paul is addressing in this discourse. They are the wild olive branches, grafted into the people of God quite against nature! In reality, you couldn't do that in antiquity with success.

The metaphor, of course, suggests an ongoing people of God, into which some Gentiles have been grafted, and some Jews have been temporarily broken off. Paul believes there has always only been one people of God, but notice how he is careful not to call this new hybrid entity "Israel." He reserves that term for non-Christian Israel throughout Romans 9–11.

Paul is administering a humility pill to his audience, reminding them: (1) you are the ones grafted in late in the game; (2) the Jewish root is what is nourishing and supporting you; (3) don't go bragging about those broken off in order to include you, because if God broke off some of the natural branches, he can break you off too; and (4) you stand by faith, and they were broken off due to unbelief. It is faith that determines whether you are a part of the tree or not.

In both verses 21 and 22, Paul warns the Gentile Christians very clearly that they must continue in faith and in God's kindness or they also will be cut off. Paul is saying you are not eternally secure, until you are securely in eternity. Short of that one stands by faith alone. And again at verse 24, Paul reminds the Gentile believers that if even they could be grafted into God's tree, how much more readily can and will the natural branches be grafted back in once more! This leveling argument is much like earlier ones in Romans where Paul wanted to make clear that Jews and Gentiles are equally indebted to the grace of God.

1. Does Paul see the people of God as a continuous unit of people, or does he believe there are two peoples of God?

2. What do you think Paul is referring to when he says the root supports and nourishes the branches? Who constitutes the root?

3. Consider this passage in light of the temptation of Christians to look down upon sinners as if from a lofty place. Stay humble and confess if necessary!

FIVE

All Israel Will Be Saved

Romans 11:25–36 RSV *Lest you be wise in your own conceits, I want you to understand this mystery, brethren: a hardening has come upon part of Israel, until the full number of the Gentiles come in, *[26]*and so all Israel will be saved; as it is written, "The Deliverer will come from Zion, he will banish ungodliness from Jacob"; *[27]*"and this will be my covenant with them when I take away their sins."*

*[28]*As regards the gospel they are enemies of God, for your sake; but as regards election they are beloved for the sake of their forefathers. *[29]*For the gifts and the call of God are irrevocable. *[30]*Just as you were once disobedient to God*

but now have received mercy because of their disobedience, ³¹so they have now been disobedient in order that by the mercy shown to you they also may receive mercy. ³²For God has consigned all men to disobedience, that he may have mercy upon all.

³³O the depth of the riches and wisdom and knowledge of God! How unsearchable are his judgments and how inscrutable his ways! ³⁴"For who has known the mind of the Lord, or who has been his counselor?" ³⁵"Or who has given a gift to him that he might be repaid?" ³⁶For from him and through him and to him are all things. To him be glory for ever. Amen.

Understanding the Word. This difficult and complex passage has been much debated by scholars. Paul begins by indicating that he is convinced the audience of Gentile Christians is ignorant of what he is about to unveil. He calls it a *musterion*, by which he means "an apocalyptic secret which God from time to time unveils to his prophets"—like Paul (see 1 Corinthians 14). He says he is revealing this so these Gentiles will not be wise in their own eyes, so they won't be conceited.

Then Paul remarks that a hardening has come on a part of Israel (see Commentary Notes), but only until the full number of Gentiles come into the people of God. The next verse, 26, can be read in one of two ways. It could be read as (A) "and thus, all Israel will be saved." This would mean that Paul sees the full inclusion of Gentiles as the saving of all Israel. So God's plan was: (1) to save a few Jews who believed in Jesus, and then (2) save a large number of Gentiles and this would be the full lot of God's people, all Israel. Or it could be read as (B) "and in the like manner, all Israel will be saved," which would mean that in the same manner as the full number of Gentiles is saved (by grace through faith in Jesus) so also a large number of Israelites will also be saved in the end. The problem with the first interpretation is that it goes against various statements Paul has already made, making clear that non-Christian Israel has not stumbled so as to fall permanently, or that they have only temporarily been broken off from the olive branch community of biblical faith. There is a further problem with the first view: it does not comport with what follows in Romans 11:26ff, as we shall see. The phrase "all Israel" is used both in the Old Testament and in the Mishnah to mean a large number of Jews (see 1 Samuel 7:5; 25:1; 1 Kings 12:1; 2 Chronicles 12:1; Daniel 9:11; Jub. 50:9; and Mishnah

San. 10:1). It does not mean every last Jew regardless of whether they finally have faith in Jesus or not.

Paul then offers a combination quotation to back up this last part of his argument, a quoting of Isaiah 59:20–21; 27:9, and then Jeremiah 31:33–34. Paul sees this as a reference to the return of Christ. He is the redeemer who will come forth from heavenly Zion and "banish godlessness away from Jacob," which must clearly refer to non-Christian Israel. The word "godlessness" is unlikely to have been used if Paul meant either saved Gentiles or saved Jews like himself. No, Paul is talking about an eschatological reversal and an eschatological miracle. Jews had traditionally believed "all Israel [would] be saved" and stream to Zion when the Messiah came, and Gentiles would come along on their coattails. Paul has exactly reversed this expectation, saying the full number of Gentiles will be saved first, and then all Israel. Finally, just before the closing doxology, Paul explains that God consigned all fallen persons over to disobedience so that he could have mercy on one and all. The Gentiles received mercy as a result of most of Israel's disobedience, and Israel will receive mercy in spite of their current disobedience, because God still loves them for the sake of the patriarchs, and God does not renege on his promises—the gifts and the call of Israel are irrevocable. This should have for once and all shut the mouth of any Gentile Christian who wanted to suggest God had left behind his first chosen people. The final doxology celebrates the wisdom and understanding of God, whose ways and judgments are past all figuring out when it comes to matters like these, but Paul has given it his best shot. One final note: the theme of mercy enunciated here at the end of Romans 11 repeatedly will recur immediately at the beginning of chapter 12, as we shall see. This is because Pauline ethics are grounded and based in Pauline theology.

1. Why is Paul revealing this mystery to the Gentiles?

2. What do you think the phrase "all Israel" means?

3. As we end this week, what questions has this study brought to mind? Consider writing or journaling around those questions.

COMMENTARY NOTES

Day 5, verse 25. Romans 11:25a presents us with a difficulty in translation. Should we render it "Israel has received a partial hardening" or "part of Israel has received a hardening?" There is a big difference between these two translations, and either seems possible. The first word in the Greek phrase is "hardening" and it literally reads "hardening in part (or to a part) to Israel until the full number of Gentiles come in." Taking into account what Paul has previously said about a remnant of grace it makes sense that he is talking about a real hardening that has happened to a part, the largest part of Israel, but it is only *pro tempore* (for a time). It is not permanent, because the next phrase clearly says, "*until* the full number of Gentiles comes in."

Day 5, verse 26. Another key technical issue is the meaning of the Greek word *houtos* in Romans 11:26. This word can be either an adverb or an adjective, but here surely it is an adverb modifying the verb "saved." As the lexicons will tell you, the meaning of *houtos* as an adverb is "in this way" or "in the same way/manner" or "thusly" or even "thus." One of the first three renderings is surely more likely here, as Paul is comparing how all Israel will be saved with how the wild olive branches (i.e., the Gentiles) have and are being saved. And the argument concludes with the assertion that God has shut up all under his mercy, and the way he did that is by breaking off Jews from the tree so that they could be regrafted into the tree on the very same basis by which Gentiles entered the tree of the people of God. There is the further possibility that we must take into account—the conjunction of *kai* with *houtos*, in which case the phrase together has a temporal sense meaning "and thereafter," so indicating that the saving of Israel will come after the saving of the full number of Gentiles.

Day 5, verse 31. In verse 31 we have a further textual issue. Should the word "now" (*nun*) be included as original to this verse or not? A preponderance of early and diverse witnesses support the omission of this word, which if original would mean that Paul thought "all Israel" was being saved on his watch, in his day, something that he does not think, as the rest of Romans 9–11 shows.

WEEK EIGHT

GATHERING DISCUSSION OUTLINE

A. Open session in prayer.

B. View video for this week's readings.

C. What general impressions and thoughts do you have after considering the video and reading and the daily writings on these Scriptures?

D. Discuss questions based on the daily readings.

    1. **KEY OBSERVATION:** When you are dealing with an argument as complex as Romans 9–11, it is wise to read through the text *as a whole* multiple times before dealing with one verse or paragraph.

       DISCUSSION QUESTION: Why is it important to read the text as a whole?

    2. **KEY OBSERVATION:** Paul is arguing in a manner that Jewish Christians would recognize and appreciate, but which Gentile Christians would likely come to realize shows that they do not know enough about the Old Testament.

       DISCUSSION QUESTION: Do you think most Christians today are just like the Gentile Christians in Rome who did not know enough about the Old Testament?

    3. **KEY OBSERVATION:** One of the major metaphors used to describe the people of God is that they are like an olive tree, perhaps the most common kind of tree one could find in the Holy Land. Paul stretches his metaphor to talk about natural and wild olive branches.

DISCUSSION QUESTION: What important truth does Paul communicate to his audience through this metaphor?

4. **KEY OBSERVATION:** Here in chapter 10 and elsewhere in the book of Romans (see Week Eleven) Paul quotes from the prophet Isaiah.

DISCUSSION QUESTION: Why do you think Paul chooses to quote often from the prophet Isaiah?

5. **KEY OBSERVATION:** At the beginning of chapter 11 Paul shows that he is proud of his Jewish heritage.

DISCUSSION QUESTION: Why do you think God chose a Jew like Paul to be apostle to the Gentiles?

E. What facts and information presented in the commentary portion of the lesson help you understand the weekly Scripture?

F. Close session with prayer.

WEEK NINE

Romans 12:1–21

Be Transformed

INTRODUCTION

Paul has now made his cognitive case, both positive and negative, for the way he presents the gospel and why he says it's all about the righteousness of God, but the acts of persuasion are far from done. Paul needs to apply the wisdom he has been dispensing; show the ethical implications of this gospel for both the Jew and the Gentile; and urge the audience to change some of their behavior in the near future, indeed before Paul arrives in Rome.

Paul's ethics are theological ethics. The imperatives are founded and grounded in the indicatives—the news of what God has been doing to save the world. This is why, at the very outset of chapter 12, Paul says that his pleading and persuading is based on what he has just been extolling—the mercies of God (cf. 11:31–32 to 12:1). Ethics in the gospel look different from ethics in the Old Testament or in the Greco-Roman world in some key respects. For one thing, the Jesus movement is not a movement involving priests, temples, and literal sacrifices, which was the essence of most all other ancient religions. Paul, like the other writers of the New Testament, will take such language and use it to refer to other ethical tasks such as, "offer your bodies as a living sacrifice." It is not helpful to simply call this spiritualizing or internalizing the terminology because Paul is calling the audience to actions, to bodily deeds, not just to spiritual attitudes or merely spiritual exercises or rituals, as we shall see. Christian praxis involves everyday interpersonal behavior as well as how one relates to God.

ONE

The Presupposition and Preamble

Romans 12:1–2 *Therefore, I urge you, brothers and sisters, in view of God's mercy, to offer your bodies as a living sacrifice, holy and pleasing to God—this is your true and proper worship. ²Do not conform to the pattern of this world, but be transformed by the renewing of your mind. Then you will be able to test and approve what God's will is—his good, pleasing and perfect will.*

Understanding the Word. Romans 12:1–2, and to a certain extent the rest of chapter 12, lay down some fundamental ethical principles on which the exhortations that follow in chapters 13–15 are based. Notice that Paul pleads earnestly with the audience on the basis of what he has already said, namely an explanation of the mercies of God. Paul is saying "in light of what a merciful God has already done to save you, you should do the following . . ."

The first step is "to offer your bodies as a living sacrifice." Not offer *something* as a sacrifice, but rather to lay yourself on the altar and offer yourself up to God, just as Abraham did with Isaac. Of course, the problem with living sacrifices is that they tend to crawl off the altar, and this is just as true of humans as of animals. In principle, we agree we should give our whole selves to God. In practice, we tend to want to reserve something of ourselves for ourselves, or our family, or our friends, and so on. But if God has actually truly, totally offered up his Son on a cross for us, then how can we not present ourselves as living sacrifices? Notice that this is not the same request as "take up your cross and follow me to Golgotha." This is not a call here, in the first instance, to martyrdom. Rather, it is a call to daily and continually offer our whole selves to God. And the offering needs to be holy and pleasing to God. God wants the best we have to offer, not our leftovers, and not our junk.

The next clause has various ways it can be translated; for instance, it could read, "for this is our logical service" or, as the old King James Version has it, "which is your reasonable service." But since Paul is talking about sacrifices, he is referring to worship, and the Greek word *latreia* can certainly refer to a religious service, and therefore worship. Think about what Paul is saying: your giving of your whole self regularly to God is worship, true and proper. Simple, normal, mundane participation in a worship service is not enough. You offering yourself to God is real worship. And, of course, you can do that either when the body of Christ gathers, or even when you are alone with God. It has been rightly said that all that we say and do should be doxological, offered up to God in praise. And if there is something we are doing which *can't* be offered up to God in praise, we should not be doing it. Once we understand worship, and what God desires and requires of us, then we begin to understand ethics. Worship is the foundation of ethics.

Verse 2 speaks of just the opposite of what verse 1 does. If verse 1 tells us the most fundamental thing a Christian should *do*, verse 2 tells us what we must *not* do. I like the rendering of the key clause here: "don't let the world around you squeeze you into its own mold" (PHILLIPS). Rather than being *conformed* to the patterns and dictates of this world, we are instead *transformed* through the renewal of our minds. The renewed mind, a mind well-grounded in the Word and will of God, is able to do the right sort of critical thinking about the world and what it offers. Notice Paul is in no way suggesting that the Christians in Rome should withdraw from engagement with the world, and live a cloistered existence. To the contrary, he wants them to live in the world without being of the world, without letting the world squeeze them into its way of thinking and patterns of living. Paul says that the renewed mind is able to sift the wheat from the chaff of the existing culture and test and then approve what God's perfect will is whilst living in the fallen world.

1. What is a living sacrifice?

2. What exactly is God's good and pleasing and perfect will? What does God want from his people?

3. What would offering your whole self to God continually require?

TWO

Each in Accordance with the Measure of His Faith

Romans 12:3–8 *For by the grace given me I say to every one of you: Do not think of yourself more highly than you ought, but rather think of yourself with*

sober judgment, in accordance with the faith God has distributed to each of you.
⁴For just as each of us has one body with many members, and these members do
not all have the same function, ⁵so in Christ we, though many, form one body,
and each member belongs to all the others. ⁶We have different gifts, according to
the grace given to each of us. If your gift is prophesying, then prophesy in accor-
dance with your faith; ⁷if it is serving, then serve; if it is teaching, then teach; ⁸if it
is to encourage, then give encouragement; if it is giving, then give generously; if it
is to lead, do it diligently; if it is to show mercy, do it cheerfully.

Understanding the Word. Somewhere between the two evils of false pride
and false humility is what Paul calls "sober judgment." It is odd, but all too
common for Christians to lean either too far to the negative in their self-
evaluation or too far to the positive. This is why Paul says that we should, on
the one hand, not think more highly of ourselves than we ought to do, but
on the other hand, not to think too little of ourselves than we ought to. False
humility is useless and not to be commended. Pretending that you can't do
anything well, or that you have no gifts to offer to God, will not do! Paul, in
fact, suggests that we should evaluate ourselves on the basis of the good gifts
that God has given each one of us.

Paul will use in this very passage the phrase "in accordance with the faith
God has distributed to each of you." What the text literally says is, "judge with
a sound mind . . . as God divided into parts the measure of faith." What Paul
means, in part, is that we should recognize what the various gifts are that God
has given this person and that person, realizing that gifts are not given for our
private benefit, but for the good of the body of Christ. Paul, once more (see
1 Corinthians 12), draws an analogy between the physical body and its various
parts that have varying functions, and the body of Christ. Our gifts belong
not to ourselves, but to the body, the collective group of believers of which
we are a part. Notice as well that Paul insists that the gifts have been given for
the common good, and indeed our gifts are "according to the grace given to
each of us," not frankly according to our desires, or wants, or even necessarily
our requests. The Holy Spirit, as 1 Corinthians 12 says, decides who gets what
gifts, and they are all meant to serve the common good. Getting and having
spiritual gifts is not like going to the grocery store and picking something out.
It is God's Spirit who decides about the distribution of gifts.

In verse 6, Paul makes a crucial statement: "if your gift is prophesying, then prophesy in accordance with your faith." Some scholars have resisted the idea that some people have more faith and some have less, but the New Testament is clear about this. So, for example, the term Jesus regularly used of his disciples in Matthew is, "you of little faith" (see Matthew 8:26; 14:31; 16:8), and this is contrasted with what he said about a Gentile centurion or a Syrophoenecian woman who were said to be of great faith. Paul is simply saying, "don't out punt your coverage," to use a football metaphor; or, to put it a different way, "don't try to go beyond the measure of your gifting." He seems to envision a prophet who becomes too enamored with his gift so that what he says is 80 percent inspiration but 20 percent perspiration, prophesying beyond the degree of inspiration, and beyond the measure of his gifting and his faith. The same applies to the use of other gifts.

Please note that this short list of gifts—prophesying, serving, teaching, encouraging, giving generously, ruling, or leading—is not meant to be exhaustive, as a quick comparison with another list or two in 1 Corinthians 12 will show. Notice that Paul is as concerned with how one exercises one's gifts and whether one does so. He says if your gift is giving, then do it generously; if your gift is leading then do it diligently; if your gift is showing mercy, then do it cheerfully. In each case, one should exercise one's gift according to the grace that has been given, and according to the measure of one's faith.

1. What does the phrase "in accordance with the faith God has distributed to each of you" mean to you?

2. What sort of gifts do you believe God has graced you with, and what are you doing with them?

3. Which way do you tend to lean in your self-evaluation; too far to the negative or too far to the positive? Pray for sober judgment.

THREE

Practice Hospitality

Romans 12:9–13 *Love must be sincere. Hate what is evil; cling to what is good.* *¹⁰Be devoted to one another in love. Honor one another above yourselves. ¹¹Never* *be lacking in zeal, but keep your spiritual fervor, serving the Lord. ¹²Be joyful in hope, patient in affliction, faithful in prayer. ¹³Share with the Lord's people who are in need. Practice hospitality.*

Understanding the Word. Beginning with verse 9, Paul offers a series of brief injunctions or imperatives, the goal of which is to convey an overall picture of what the character and behavior of a Christian ought to be like. First off, and of first importance, Paul talks about love (*agape*, not *eros*). He says that love must be genuine or sincere. The word translated "sincere" is the antonym of the Greek word for "play-acting" or "hypocritical." But, in fact, the Greek is so telegraphic and clipped that some of these injunctions need to be taken together. The first one reads literally "the love must be sincere, hating the evil, clinging to the good." Then, in verse 10, he speaks of brotherly or sisterly love, saying, "be devoted to one another in love." He adds, "honor one another above yourselves."

Paul then adds, "never be lacking in zeal, but keep your spiritual fervor." Paul is not an advocate of tepid or lukewarm Christianity. But this spiritual fervor, zeal, and earnestness must be expressed in the cause of serving the Lord Jesus, not in the way Paul expressed when he was Saul, the persecutor of the church.

The phrases become even more clipped: "be joyful in hope, patient in affliction, faithful in prayer." The Christian virtues are often counterintuitive. They are not natural responses to difficulties in life. The Christian is called to be proactive, not reactive to his circumstances. Verse 13 concludes this subsection with, "share with the Lord's people who are in need." We have here the participial form of the familiar word *koinonia*, which does not mean "fellowship," but is an active word meaning "participating (or sharing) in common with someone in something" and all the more so here when we have a participial imperative. Finally, he adds, "practice hospitality," or pursue or aim at *zenophilia*. This word literally means, "the love of strangers" (or even aliens; i.e., foreigners). It came to be the typical word for "hospitality." One was to show hospitality even to strangers, those one does not know. Notice then how Paul insists the real Christian will do good to all persons, including but not limited to the household of faith. Some Christians help their fellow Christians, but do not practice "hospitality" according to the natural meaning of this word—welcoming, serving, feeding, and sheltering strangers.

1. Paul refers to several sorts of love in this paragraph. What are the differences between agape and brotherly or sisterly love, and the love of strangers or foreigners?

2. Paul also calls for authenticity and fervency. Why do you think so many Christians fall into various sorts of hypocrisy even to the point of hiding their real loyalties at work or in the public sphere?

3. What would it mean for you to be proactive rather than reactive in difficult circumstances? Consider journaling about a difficulty you face.

FOUR
Following Jesus

Romans 12:14–16 *Bless those who persecute you; bless and do not curse. ¹⁵Rejoice with those who rejoice; mourn with those who mourn. ¹⁶Live in harmony with one another. Do not be proud, but be willing to associate with people of low position. Do not be conceited.*

Understanding the Word. Here, and elsewhere in Romans 12–14, it becomes quite clear that Paul knows at least some of Jesus' teachings that we find in the Sermon on the Mount in Matthew 5–7, and he applies them to Gentile as well as Jewish Christians in Rome. So it is that Christians are to "bless those who persecute [them]," rather than curse them. Then, reciting a form of the Beatitudes, Paul says "rejoice with those who rejoice" and "mourn with those who mourn." Blessing a persecutor is going in the opposite direction to the emotions being expressed by the persecutor, whereas empathizing with the mourning or rejoicing is, of course, sharing in the emotions of those who grieve or celebrate.

Verse 16 is interesting. It says, "live in harmony with one another," which is then qualified by, "do not be proud, but be willing to associate with people of low position." Humility was not a virtue in the Greco-Roman world. Indeed, the usual word for this quality meant "craven" or "acting like a slave," which is something to which no free person in Rome would aspire. No elite or free Gentile was taught to think like a servant of others. Humility is not primarily an attitude about one's self, and it certainly isn't feelings of low self-worth. If

Jesus was the model of true humility, it can't have anything to do with feelings of low self-worth. If there was one person who walked this earth who knew clearly and fully his sacred worth and abilities, it was Jesus. In fact, it is mostly an action word. Humility is the posture of a strong person, stepping down and serving others self-sacrificingly just as is described of the actions of Christ in Philippians 2:5–11.

Humility and forgiveness were two unusual or distinctive traits cultivated by Christians (and also before them by Jews). In short, Paul is touting virtues that would not be advocated by Seneca or Epictetus or other pagan ethicists of the period. The last phrase in this section underscores the distinctive Christian ethic: "don't get a swelled head about yourself" or "don't be thinking so highly of yourself" (i.e., "do not be conceited").

1. Paul's ethic presupposes the aid of the Spirit. To what degree would you say this ethic is counterintuitive to a non-Christian person who wants to protect themselves and get ahead in life?

2. What does "humility" amount to and mean?

3. Are you regularly willing to "associate with people of low position"?

FIVE

No Payback; Overcome Evil with Good

Romans 12:17–21 *Do not repay anyone evil for evil. Be careful to do what is right in the eyes of everyone. 18If it is possible, as far as it depends on you, live at peace with everyone. 19Do not take revenge, my dear friends, but leave room for God's wrath, for it is written: "It is mine to avenge; I will repay," says the Lord. 20On the contrary: "If your enemy is hungry, feed him; if he is thirsty, give him something to drink. In doing this, you will heap burning coals on his head." 21Do not be overcome by evil, but overcome evil with good.*

Understanding the Word. Undergirding the ethic of this section of chapter 12 is the principle that God is the just judge of the world, and we are not, and so we should leave justice and vengeance and the meting out of judgment in God's hands, and not try to do it ourselves. This principle works out in practice to mean: (1) "do not repay anyone evil for evil"; (2) "be careful to do what is right in the eyes of everyone"; (3) "as far as it depends on you, live at peace with everyone"; (4) "do not take revenge [. . .] but leave room for God's wrath" to sort out injustices and wrongs. (Deuteronomy 32:35 is quoted here, Yahweh saying he will repay.)

This advice goes completely against the grain of the rivalry conventions and the reciprocity conventions of the ancient world. Paul lived in a payback world, both in the positive sense ("you scratch my back and I'll scratch yours") and in the negative sense as well ("you harm me, and I will escalate the damage against you"). Families were in competition with one another for honor, and property, and status, and so on. The culture was competitive, dog-eat-dog, and did not practice forgiveness. Into that environment Paul offers this countercultural ethic—and make no mistake, this was absolutely a countercultural ethic—and, frankly, still is today in most senses.

Instead, says Paul, "kill them with kindness," and he quotes Proverbs 25:21–22. Verse 21 sums up Paul's core advice as an alternative to taking revenge—namely, "do not be overcome by evil, but overcome evil with good." Or as one bumper sticker says: "Love your enemies. It will at least confuse them." Paul seems, in fact, to suggest it will make them feel guilty.

1. What is the hardest part about this ethic of nonviolence and love that Paul is advocating?

2. How much do you think Paul the persecutor had to change to be such an advocate of this sort of ethic?

3. Do you think we still live in a payback world? Do you ever struggle with wanting to take revenge?

COMMENTARY NOTES

General Comments. The ethical injunctions in Paul's letters seem to presume a lot of the audience. In this particular grouping of diverse imperatives, Paul is not only drawing on the Jesus tradition from the Sermon on the Mount, he is also drawing on Old Testament sources like Proverbs. One would normally expect that only the Jewish members in the audience would pick up some of these signals and allusions, or perhaps some Gentiles who had formerly been God-fearers and had attended the synagogue. It would appear that Paul is assuming that there is a critical mass of more mature knowledgeable Christians in Rome who can unpack these elliptical and brief exhortations. In fact, of course, when we get to Romans 16 we discover that some of Paul's regular coworkers, Priscilla and Aquila, and also Andronicus and Junia, who are apostles and Pauline coworkers, are there, and could help with explanations. In early Judaism the focus seems mainly to have been on orthopraxy, on behavior, not on orthodoxy. This is one of the things that makes the fledgling Christian movement stand out from early Judaism—the huge quantity of theological reflection (see Romans 1–11) to which is added more brief advice about behavior. This surely would have struck Gentile listeners as more like the rhetorical and philosophical discourses they heard at symposiums after dining in someone's house.

WEEK NINE

GATHERING DISCUSSION OUTLINE

A. Open session in prayer.

B. View video for this week's readings.

C. What general impressions and thoughts do you have after considering the video and reading and the daily writings on these Scriptures?

D. Discuss questions based on the daily readings.

1. **KEY OBSERVATION:** When one gets to chapters 12–15 it is obvious that the Christians in Rome are not a unified *ekklesia* (church) and, even worse, they are divided along ethnic lines—the Jewish Christians largely not meeting with the Gentile Christians.

   DISCUSSION QUESTION: What do you think Paul's ethical advice is intended to do?

2. **KEY OBSERVATION:** Sometimes it is said of the ethic of Jesus that it presents us with an ideal that no one could really live up to. Paul does not agree.

   DISCUSSION QUESTION: How does Paul think kingdom ethics can be lived up to?

3. **KEY OBSERVATION:** The ethical seriousness of early Christianity is notable. Obedience is required, not optional. When Paul refers to the obedience of faith, he is talking about a pattern of behavior, which if not followed, can indeed impede one's growth in grace.

DISCUSSION QUESTION: Do you agree with Paul that ethics are a necessary working out of one's salvation and sanctification?

4. **KEY OBSERVATION:** As we have seen, Paul's ethical advice goes countercultural to the ethics of his day.

   DISCUSSION QUESTION: What would the Christian community to whom Paul is writing look like if they obeyed to the letter what Paul says they should do?

5. **KEY OBSERVATION:** It needs to be stressed that the ethic Paul is enunciating is an ethic for Christians and the Christian community, not for governments or other public institutions.

   DISCUSSION QUESTION: What are some presuppositions that make this ethic Christian-specific?

E. What facts and information presented in the commentary portion of the lesson help you understand the weekly Scripture?

F. Close session with prayer.

WEEK TEN

Romans 13:1–14:23

Rules to Live By

INTRODUCTION

In Romans 13–14, Paul continues with his ethical exhortations and, as in Romans 12, he is briefly touching on a variety of ethical topics. The teaching comes across as more of a reminder than a breaking of new ground. Since the majority of the Roman Christians are not his own converts, he is providing a broad basis of ethical teaching, as he did earlier in the discourse with his theological teaching, drawing out the ethical implications of the gospel about the righteousness of God. God, in Paul's view, is not just interested in setting people back into a right relationship with himself, he is also interested in their modeling the righteous character of their Maker as well, and even more particularly the loving, self-sacrificial, forgiving, and non-violent character of Jesus. Lest we think that Paul is simply offering up a short and general course in Christian ethics for everyone, without any specific situations in Rome in mind (especially in chapters 14 and 15), it will become apparent that this is not the case.

ONE

Submit to the Governing Authorities

Romans 13:1–7 RSV *Let every person be subject to the governing authorities. For there is no authority except from God, and those that exist have been instituted by God. ²Therefore he who resists the authorities resists what God has appointed, and those who resist will incur judgment. ³For rulers are not a terror to good conduct, but to bad. Would you have no fear of him who is* *in authority? Then do what is good, and you will receive his approval, ⁴for he is God's servant for your good. But if you do wrong, be afraid, for he does not bear the sword in vain; he is the servant of God to execute his wrath on the wrongdoer. ⁵Therefore one must be subject, not only to avoid God's wrath but also for the sake of conscience. ⁶For the same reason you also pay taxes, for the authorities are ministers of God, attending to this very thing. ⁷Pay all of them their dues, taxes to whom taxes are due, revenue to whom revenue is due, respect to whom respect is due, honor to whom honor is due.*

Understanding the Word. Paul's basic principle when it comes to ethics is: live at peace with everyone, offering no offense, except the inherent offense of the gospel and its necessary implications (both theological and ethical). It is not a surprise that someone who is a Roman citizen would not be a revolutionary when it comes to the issue of government and taxes. At the same time, it must be kept clearly in mind that what Paul says here in Romans 13:1–7 presupposes government on its best behavior, not one like the madness of Nero (AD 64) or like the demonic character and brutal policies of Domitian (AD 81–96). The Christian response to government must depend on the character of the governing (and of the laws, of course). Here Paul councils a response that should allow Christians to be left alone by the governmental authorities. What should especially be stressed here is that Christianity was not at this point a *religio licita*, "a legal or licit religion." It was not on the approved list, so to speak, unlike Judaism. Once it became clear that the Jesus movement was not just a further sect of Judaism, there was real danger for the movement. It would be classed as a new "superstition," and could possibly be banned from Rome. Indeed, the actions of Claudius in the late 40s exiling various Jewish Christian leaders from Rome had to be taken as a warning sign of possible future trouble. When the Christians returned to Rome in AD 54, they needed to do their best to live at peace with both their Gentile and Jewish neighbors, and simply get on with the positive living out of the Christian life. Paul writes with all this in mind.

Paul opens by saying that Christians should submit to the governing authorities (of whatever rank), because no genuine authority exists except as it comes from God. This, of course, is based in the basic Old Testament notion that it is God who raises up rulers and puts them down. It is, however, probably important that Paul uses the verb "be subject to" here, which could be distinguished from "obey." There would be times that Christians could not obey this or that law of a pagan government, but they could still recognize the authority of the government by submitting to its jurisprudence.

As this paragraph progresses, it becomes apparent that Paul is indeed talking about government at its best, working for the public good, not a terror to anyone except lawbreakers, only enforcing the law by force when necessary, and so on. Christianity did not entail, in Paul's view, a rejection of all human government as wicked. Paul is actually saying that the authorities that exist have been established by God and that we should submit to them. If a Christian is a law-abiding citizen and does what is good, he may even be commended by the authorities. All those in authority are seen as servants of God. This, of course, comports with Paul's larger view of God's sovereignty over all things, and God's hands-on approach to human history, especially when it comes to issues affecting God's people.

If we are wondering how Paul might reconcile verse 4—the statement about governments bearing the sword where necessary and what Paul says about Christians avoiding violence against other human beings altogether—the answer is relatively clear. Paul is assuming Christians will not take on roles in society that could involve the use of lethal force. This is indeed why various Christians in the first centuries of church history: (1) could not in good conscience serve in the Roman army, and (2) could not be a governing official that from time to time used violence to enforce the law—say a police officer or a tax collector. Christians could play other roles in society, but not these. This is the sort of delicate dance Christians had to perform to remain in the world without being of the world, and still steadfastly following the ethic enunciated by Jesus in the Sermon on the Mount, and later by Paul in Romans 12–15 and elsewhere. Thus Paul insists in verse 5 that it is necessary to submit to the governing authorities not just for fear of punishment, but as a matter of conscience. Christians are to "seek [the welfare] the peace and prosperity of the city" as God himself through the prophet Jeremiah said, referring to pagan governments that would rule over the Jews in exile (Jer. 29:7).

Paul is not an early advocate of the Tea Party's views on taxes either. He says in verse 6 that believers should pay them to keep the government running and providing the protection and services it does. Finally, Christians are called to give honor, respect, and taxes to those to whom such things are due. In fact, at the beginning of the next subsection of the exhortation, Paul will say we should owe no one anything except love.

1. What is Paul's basic view of government when it is operating properly and justly?

2. Why is it said that the ethic of Jesus is just an ethic for his followers, not for those who are not his followers?

3. What do you think of Paul's assumption that Christians will not take on roles in society that could involve use of lethal force?

TWO
Eschatological Ethics

Romans 13:8–14 RSV *Owe no one anything, except to love one another; for he who loves his neighbor has fulfilled the law. ⁹The commandments, "You shall not commit adultery, You shall not kill, You shall not steal, You shall not covet," and any other commandment, are summed up in this sentence, "You shall love your neighbor as yourself." ¹⁰Love does no wrong to a neighbor; therefore love is the fulfilling of the law.*

¹¹Besides this you know what hour it is, how it is full time now for you to wake from sleep. For salvation is nearer to us now than when we first believed; ¹²the night is far gone, the day is at hand. Let us then cast off the works of darkness and put on the armor of light; ¹³let us conduct ourselves becomingly as in the day, not in reveling and drunkenness, not in debauchery and licentiousness, not in quarreling and jealousy. ¹⁴But put on the Lord Jesus Christ, and make no provision for the flesh, to gratify its desires.

Understanding the Word. It has been rightly said that Pauline ethics are eschatological in character, meaning they are definitely affected by and require keeping one eye on the horizon for the possible imminent return of Christ. Of course, it is also true that they are grounded in what God has already accomplished in Christ, which has begun the eschatological age. Like Paul's theology, his ethics have an already-and-not-yet character to them.

Paul stresses from verses 8–10 that if you really live out the implications of Christian love, which includes love of neighbor (whether Christian or not), then you will have fulfilled the listed Ten Commandments. Paul is not saying love is an alternative to avoiding adultery, murder, etc. He is saying that the real implications of loving thy neighbor includes avoiding all such sins, and so is a fulfillment of these other commandments as well. You may notice that Paul does not also say keeping the Sabbath is one of the commandments that is fulfilled by love, and specifically love of neighbor. In fact, the Sabbath commandment is the one commandment of the Ten Commandments that neither Jesus nor Paul required of the followers of Jesus, as we shall see in examining chapter 14. In addition, Paul believes not only that "love does no wrong to a neighbor," but that, in fact, love seeks the well-being of the neighbor. The ethic of love involves not just nonviolence but positive goodwill toward all.

Verses 11–14 provide what is called the eschatological sanction for the ethics, by which is meant, "you need to behave in this way because we are already in the end times and you never know when Jesus may return and require an accounting of your behavior." Paul means that the eschatological clock has already been set ticking, and final salvation is nearer now than when the audience first believed. It seems clear enough that Paul, without giving way to any sort of predictions or prognostications, conjures up the idea of the possible imminence of the return of Christ, hence the need for Christians to be ethically serious and always ready to meet their Maker. For texts like 1 Thessalonians 5, where Paul uses the "Christ will come like a thief in the night" metaphor, we understand that Paul means Christ will return at an unknown time; it could be much later, but it could also be soon, and therefore Christians must follow the Boy Scout motto: "be prepared."

Paul develops the metaphor here of the return of Christ being like the dawn of the sun in the morning, and so he tells the audience it's time to both give up the deeds of darkness, the wicked deeds one tends to do under the cloak of darkness, and instead wake up and behave decently as one would normally do during the daytime (i.e., avoiding carousing, sexual immorality, debauchery in general, and avoiding the sort of arguments and fights that are caused by drunkenness). Instead, the wide-awake Christian is to get up, put on his Christ-clothes, and not even think about gratifying the sinful inclinations.

1. What is the heart of the Christian ethic that Paul refers to here?

2. What is meant by the eschatological sanction of Pauline ethics?

3. What would it mean to "cast off the works of darkness and put on the armor of light" and to "put on the Lord Jesus Christ" today? Consider journaling on this.

THREE

The Weak and the Strong

Romans 14:1–4 RSV *As for the man who is weak in faith, welcome him, but not for disputes over opinions.* *²One believes he may eat anything, while the weak man eats only vegetables.* *³Let not him who eats despise him who abstains, and let not him who abstains pass judgment on him who eats; for God has welcomed him.* *⁴Who are you to pass judgment on the servant of another? It is before his own master that he stands or falls. And he will be upheld, for the Master is able to make him stand.*

Understanding the Word. At last we begin to sense some of the real problems in the Roman community of Christians. What is interesting is that here, as in 1 Corinthians 8–10, Paul calls the person who has too *many* scruples about food "the weak." Paul is likely addressing Gentiles who look down on Jewish Christians who follow food laws, and apparently some of them are even strict vegetarians. There is a good reason in Rome why they might have gone that route: namely, that there were no kosher butchers and so all meat was tainted and unclean from their point of view.

Paul is insisting: (1) that there should be no quarrels over food; (2) the person with more scruples about what is appropriate to eat should not be looked down on with contempt; (3) God has accepted the one with too many scruples and the ones with few or none when it comes to food; (4) Paul is actually saying something rather revolutionary for a Jew: namely, that God has declared all food clean as did Jesus (see Acts 10 and Mark 7), and therefore even for Jews, keeping food laws is optional, but some Jewish Christians had not yet come to believe this, and they were not to be despised; (5) it is not for the Gentile Christians in Rome to judge the scrupulous Jewish ones, because they are all servants of God, not servants of the Gentiles, and as such only God has a right to evaluate persons who keep strict food laws. But this is not the only problem in Rome. There is also a problem about worship days as well, as we shall see in the next section.

What has happened with the Pauline ethic is that some things, which previously for Paul the Pharisee had been ethical requirements for being a good and godly person, had become (in his view) optional, not obligatory. Food laws, Sabbath-keeping, and circumcision were no longer required—the most salient things that set Jews apart from Christians. For Paul, food laws and Sabbath-keeping had become *adiaphora*, "things indifferent that one could either observe or not." Circumcision, however, Paul would argue strongly against for Gentiles, especially because circumcision was the covenant sign of the Mosaic covenant, and Paul did not think any Christian should submit to a covenant which was becoming obsolete and had been eclipsed by the new covenant with its own covenant sign—baptism. Obviously, the Judaizers referred to in Galatians disagreed with Paul about this matter.

1. What is surprising about Paul calling someone with scruples against eating things like meat "the weak"?

2. What is Paul's main concern in this exhortation that is meant to protect the weak?

3. How can you apply what Paul is saying here with regard to judging brothers or sisters over what might be considered nonessentials?

FOUR

Worship Wars

Romans 14:5–12 *One person considers one day more sacred than another; another considers every day alike. Each of them should be fully convinced in their own mind. *[6]*Whoever regards one day as special does so to the Lord. Whoever eats meat does so to the Lord, for they give thanks to God; and whoever abstains does so to the Lord and gives thanks to God. *[7]*For none of us lives for ourselves alone, and none of us dies for ourselves alone. *[8]*If we live, we live for the Lord; and if we die, we die for the Lord. So, whether we live or die, we belong to the Lord.*

⁹For this very reason, Christ died and returned to life so that he might be the Lord of both the dead and the living.

¹⁰You, then, why do you judge your brother or sister? Or why do you treat them with contempt? For we will all stand before God's judgment seat. ¹¹It is written: "'As surely as I live,' says the Lord, 'every knee will bow before me; every tongue will acknowledge God.'"

¹²So then, each of us will give an account of ourselves to God.

Understanding the Word. As surprising as were Paul's exhortations in the previous paragraph, here they get even more surprising. Paul says that some observe one day as the Lord's Day, and some say every day should be seen as the Lord's Day, and then he drops what would be a bombshell for Jews: "each of them should be fully convinced in their own mind." That is, it's a matter of individual conscience. So much for Sabbath-keeping required for one and all, or at least for Jewish Christians.

Paul then speaks about eating meat, and clearly he has no problem with it, as long as either eating or abstaining is done "to the Lord." The point is, that we should do all things in a way that praises and honors the Lord. Our entire lives should be doxological; whether we live or we die, we do so unto the Lord, who died for us on the cross. Paul also stresses, "none of us lives for ourselves alone" but all of us live for the Lord. Our whole lives and behavior should be christological in shape and should reflect the character and the course of ministry of Jesus, even if it involves dying for the Lord.

The conclusion of these remarks is the reminder that we should not be judging one another about these sorts of things, but rather leave judgment in the hands of God. We will all one day stand before God's judgment seat and have to give an account of the deeds done in the body (cf. verse 10 with 2 Corinthians 5:10). Paul then quotes Isaiah 45:23 to reinforce the point.

1. In what sense will Christians be judged on the day of judgment?

2. What does the principle "no Christian lives for himself alone" suggest to you in a culture where the vast majority of people, including Christians, are indeed living for themselves?

3. If doing all things in a way that praises and honors the Lord was your aim, what areas would you desire to grow in?

FIVE

Food for Thought

Romans 14:13–23 *Therefore let us stop passing judgment on one another. Instead, make up your mind not to put any stumbling block or obstacle in the way of a brother or sister. ¹⁴I am convinced, being fully persuaded in the Lord Jesus, that nothing is unclean in itself. But if anyone regards something as unclean, then for that person it is unclean. ¹⁵If your brother or sister is distressed because of what you eat, you are no longer acting in love. Do not by your eating destroy someone for whom Christ died. ¹⁶Therefore do not let what you know is good be spoken of as evil. ¹⁷For the kingdom of God is not a matter of eating and drinking, but of righteousness, peace and joy in the Holy Spirit, ¹⁸because anyone who serves Christ in this way is pleasing to God and receives human approval.*

¹⁹Let us therefore make every effort to do what leads to peace and to mutual edification. ²⁰Do not destroy the work of God for the sake of food. All food is clean, but it is wrong for a person to eat anything that causes someone else to stumble. ²¹It is better not to eat meat or drink wine or to do anything else that will cause your brother or sister to fall.

²²So whatever you believe about these things keep between yourself and God. Blessed is the one who does not condemn himself by what he approves. ²³But whoever has doubts is condemned if they eat, because their eating is not from faith; and everything that does not come from faith is sin.

Understanding the Word. Paul further develops his views on the food issue. He states firmly that his belief is that "nothing is unclean in itself." This would include food. He adds, however, that if someone regards a food as unclean, then it is unclean for them, by which he seems to mean that it would be a violation of conscience for them to eat it. It becomes clear that Paul is most concerned, however, about interpersonal behavior that puts a stumbling block—a *skandalon* from which we get the word *scandal*—or a major obstacle in the path of the overly scrupulous Christian. This behavior, in turn, scandalizes the person in question and sets up a barrier to fellowship with that person. So, "if your brother or sister is distressed [by] what you eat, [by eating it in his presence] you are no longer acting in love." The action becomes a provocation. Paul, using dramatic hyperbole, suggests that doing this could actually destroy the person's faith, a person for whom Christ died. In other words, Paul is shaming such a person into not behaving that way. He admits that eating the food is fine, but what is happening is that doing something that the strong person knows is good, becomes evil when it causes another to stumble in their walk with the Lord. This is hardly kingdom behavior, which is not constituted by demanding our rights to eat or drink something, rather than acting according the righteousness, peace, and joy the Holy Spirit is trying to produce in the body of Christ. Behaving in a way that is sensitive to other Christians and their scruples, whether you think they are valid or not, is both pleasing to God and should receive human approbation.

In other words, don't act in a selfish and self-centered way that is a sort of condemnation or judgment on those more scrupulous, because Christian ethics require that we behave in ways that are edifying and make for peace and harmony with our fellow believers. The problem is, this seems not to be happening in Rome. Toward the end of this section, Paul becomes more explicit—he says it is wrong, morally wrong, for a person to eat anything which causes another present brother or sister to stumble, not because of what sort of food it is, but because of ignoring the conscience of another and violating what counts as loving your neighbor. The real concern is that the overly scrupulous person could be caused to stumble or even fall by this sort of selfish and insensitive behavior. "Blessed is the one who does not condemn himself by what he approves" (even if there is nothing in principle wrong with eating pork barbecue). On the other hand, the Christian who can't eat some kind of food without doubts or twinges of conscience is not eating in accord with the measure of their faith, and "everything that does not come from faith is sin" at least for that person.

It is clear enough that this problem of table fellowship amongst Jewish and Gentile believers was a problem in more than one Pauline city and set of congregations (see 1 Corinthians 8–10), as Paul has to deal with the issue repeatedly. Jews and Gentiles were just beginning to learn how to have fellowship in Christ together, how to break bread together, and there were difficulties along the way. What this part of the discourse suggests is that Paul knows about the situation on the ground in the Roman churches better than his Gentile audience may have thought. Interestingly, Paul is suggesting that for a person who is overly scrupulous there seems to be a larger category of what counts as sins for them than for Christians who don't have such scruples about food, or the day of worship, or other such issues.

1. Why do you think Paul dwells on the food issue here at such length?

2. What do you make of the pronouncement that whatever you cannot do in good faith is at least a sin for you, a violation of conscience?

3. Have you ever been in a situation where something you could do in good faith would potentially cause another to stumble or vice versa?

COMMENTARY NOTES

General Comments. The Greek word *adelphos* simply means "brother," but it is clear enough in texts like Romans 14:10, 13, 15, and 21 that the term is used inclusively of both brothers and sisters in Christ. Paul is not just addressing the men in the audience. This creates a dilemma for the translator, especially if he is trying to adhere quite literally to the Greek original. Obviously, the Bible was written in an era before the concern about inclusive speech became an issue. In my judgment, it is best to translate things according to what they actually mean or refer to, not simply on the basis of what they say. They produce less confusion. Hence, I am fine with the translation "brothers and sisters" in the aforementioned places in chapter 14.

A few Greek New Testament manuscripts (for instance L and the Byzantine lectionary and some minuscles) place Romans 16:25–27 following 14:23 in Romans. Other manuscripts, in particular the early Papyrus 46, place 16:25–27 after 15:33. This has led various scholars to speculate about what might have been the original ending of Romans. Some have, in fact, concluded that chapter 15, perhaps with the addition of Romans 16:25–27, was the original ending of Romans. The vast majority of our earliest and best manuscripts do not have Romans 16:25–27 following 14:23, and do not end the manuscript here, or for that matter at the end of Romans 15 either. What may have happened however is this: (1) Romans 16 was originally a letter of introduction, a cover letter of sorts for Phoebe, which was originally a separate document to Romans 1–15; (2) then at some juncture Romans 16 was added to Romans 1–15 to keep the materials together. Against even this suggestion, however, is the fact that a normal letter often did have greetings at the conclusion of the document.

Day 1. The years AD 54–59 were considered by later Roman historians as a golden age of government. However, in AD 64 the city of Rome burned, and the then-emperor, Nero, made Christians the scapegoats for starting the fire and a severe persecution began. Again in the 90s when John wrote his apocalypse, which we call Revelation, another persecution began under Emperor Domitian whose demonic character and brutal policies were well known.

Day 1, verse 4. "for rulers to not bear the sword for no reason." In this case it seems to refer to the short sword carried for protection by the tax officers.

WEEK TEN

GATHERING DISCUSSION OUTLINE

A. Open session in prayer.

B. View video for this week's readings.

C. What general impressions and thoughts do you have after considering the video and reading and the daily writings on these Scriptures?

D. Discuss questions based on the daily readings.

1. **KEY OBSERVATION:** Despite the fact that Paul was not yet an authority figure or apostle in the Roman church, and had not yet visited it, it is noteworthy how he feels he has the authority to weigh into the ethical dilemmas plaguing that group of house churches.

    DISCUSSION QUESTION: Why do you think the Christians in Rome received Paul's message with authority even though he had not yet even visited Rome?

2. **KEY OBSERVATION:** The materials in chapters 13–14 are mainly concerned with urging Christians to behave in ways that allow the congregations to not attract negative attention from pagans or the authorities, and on the other hand to make sure that interpersonal behavior in the church gatherings was such that it promoted unity, not division.

    DISCUSSION QUESTION: Why do you think this was so important to Paul?

3. **KEY OBSERVATION:** What Romans 13–14 reveal to us is that even by the late 50s AD the ground rules for fellowship between Jewish and Gentile Christians are not written in stone.

   DISCUSSION QUESTION: Do you think some of the issues that Paul was addressing, such as what one should eat or when one should worship, continued past the time in which Romans was written?

4. **KEY OBSERVATION:** Paul's view of God's sovereignty includes, not surprisingly in light of the Old Testament, the idea that God raises up and takes down rulers of various sorts, and any genuine ruler has his authority and power ultimately from God.

   DISCUSSION QUESTION: Why do you think Paul wanted the Christians in Rome to behave toward the government in such a way that did not draw attention to themselves?

5. **KEY OBSERVATION:** For Paul the command to "love your neighbor as yourself" is paramount in the Christian ethic, and Paul is not allowing any sort of redefinitions of neighbor that excludes one people group or another.

   DISCUSSION QUESTION: How is a love that is genuine and sincere and that loves even one's enemies possible?

E. What facts and information presented in the commentary portion of the lesson help you understand the weekly Scripture?

F. Close session with prayer.

Romans 15:1–33

Paul's Reason for Writing

INTRODUCTION

At first glance, this chapter appears to be a grab bag of various sorts of materials. There are more ethical imperatives, a final peroration for Gentile Christians, travel plans, and apparently a closing benediction not once but twice, once in verse 13 and again in verse 33. What becomes clear upon close scrutiny of the material is how focused it is on addressing and speaking about Gentiles, and about Paul being the apostle to the Gentiles. To make things even more complex, Paul interrupts his final peroration, the start of which is in verses 14–21, and the emotional conclusion of which is in verses 30–33. Partly the digression is caused by Paul trying to blend epistolary and rhetorical elements together as he draws to a close. As one reads chapter 16, it becomes clear that Paul is addressing all the Jewish Christians he knows and can name in Rome, and gives them a separate concluding peroration in verses 17–20, where Paul especially addresses the "weak" amongst the Jewish Christians in Rome, just as he had addressed the "strong" Gentile Christians in chapter 15. What this makes abundantly clear is how deep the divisions are between the Jewish and Gentile Christians in Rome; so deep, as we shall see, that Paul in the end has to do something unprecedented—he tells the two groups of Christians to embrace one another with every show of affection. In particular, he urges the Gentiles to take the initiative and embrace all the people he names in Romans 16. This is a surprising kind of greeting card to say the least because elsewhere Paul simply sends greetings or receives them, but in this case it is Roman Christians who need to get on with greeting and embracing other Roman Christians.

ONE

A Word to the Wise for the Strong

Romans 15:1–6 RSV *We who are strong ought to bear with the failings of the weak, and not to please ourselves;* ²*let each of us please his neighbor for his good, to edify him.* ³*For Christ did not please himself; but, as it is written, "The reproaches of those who reproached thee fell on me."* ⁴*For whatever was written in former days was written for our instruction, that by steadfastness and by the encouragement of the scriptures we might have hope.* ⁵*May the God of steadfastness and encouragement grant you to live in such harmony with one another, in accord with Christ Jesus,* ⁶*that together you may with one voice glorify the God and Father of our Lord Jesus Christ.*

Understanding the Word. Whereas previously in Romans 14 Paul had talked about the weak and sought to protect them, here he openly identifies with the strong, but he urges that while the weak certainly have failings, the strong should bear with them and not try to impose their own practices on the weak. This is not because Paul is a modern advocate of "think and let think," but because he wants unity in the body in Rome. The goal is not to please ourselves, but to please God, and also to please our neighbors so as to build them up. Even Jesus did not seek to please himself. Paul quotes Psalm 69:9 "the insults of those who insult you have fallen on me" (NRSV). What is Paul alluding to here, besides the fact that when he was reviled, Christ did not return the abuse? Who is the "you" meant to be in the quotation? I would suggest the "you" is the weak Jewish Christians who are reviled for their food laws, etc., and the "me" is the strong, like Jesus, like Paul, who for the sake of fellowship and unity with the weak, will stand with them when they are abused, even when the strong person might disagree with their overly scrupulous attitudes and practices.

Verse 4 provides us with an interesting glimpse of Paul's view of Scripture and how it functions for Christians. The Old Testament is suitable for teaching Christians, and in this case, the lessons are teaching Christians how to endure and be encouraged so they do not stop looking forward to the future in hope. This verse ought to be compared with 2 Timothy 3:16, where something similar though more detailed is said about the function of the Old Testament for Christians. It is, however, important to understand the Pauline distinction between the Old Testament continuing to be God's Word for promoting encouragement and endurance for Christians and the keeping of the Mosaic covenant on the other hand. Paul believes Christians are not under the Mosaic law, but he still believes all of the Old Testament can instruct Christians in other ways without requiring them to keep various of the commandments that Paul sees as obsolete for the followers of Christ. Paul's view is that Christians are under a new covenant, but since God is the same God, there is plenty of overlap between the previous instructions in the old covenant and the current instructions in the new covenant.

Verses 5–6 constitute something of a benediction. It is a benediction meant to invoke the aid of God in creating a unified people of God in Rome. The Christians there need to be of one mind, they need to fellowship together, they need to worship together. They need to respect and honor one another. The word *homothymadon* (found here in verse 6) occurs in the important summaries in Acts 2 and 4 as well as elsewhere (cf. Acts 1:14; 2:46; 4:24; 5:12; 7:57) as something that characterized the mother church in Jerusalem at the outset—they were all of one mind and met together. There must be a unity if they are to meet together and praise God together. It is right to hear some echoes of the initial prayer of Paul in Romans 1:9–12 here.

1. Why do you think Paul identifies with the strong, who seem to be simply Gentiles who do not follow Jewish practices?

2. What uses does Paul say the Old Testament Scripture has for Christians?

3. Paul here speaks of the importance for Christians to be like-minded or of "one mind" about crucial things. Where do you see Christians most divided over crucial things? How might you pray over this today?

TWO

Christ—Servant of the Jews, Savior of the Gentiles

Romans 15:7–13 *Accept one another, then, just as Christ accepted you, in order to bring praise to God. ⁸For I tell you that Christ has become a servant of the Jews on behalf of God's truth, so that the promises made to the patriarchs might be confirmed ⁹and, moreover, that the Gentiles might glorify God for his mercy. As it is written: "Therefore I will praise you among the Gentiles; I will sing the praises of your name."*

¹⁰Again, it says, "Rejoice, you Gentiles, with his people."

¹¹And again, "Praise the Lord, all you Gentiles; let all the peoples extol him."

¹²And again, Isaiah says, "The Root of Jesse will spring up, one who will arise to rule over the nations; in him the Gentiles will hope."

¹³May the God of hope fill you with all joy and peace as you trust in him, so that you may overflow with hope by the power of the Holy Spirit.

Understanding the Word. Paul makes a direct appeal in verse 7 for the Christians in Rome to "accept one another, then, just as Christ accepted you." Here we have a clear sign that Paul knows that this has not, or has not sufficiently happened thus far. It should be done to the praise of a God who is for all people, Jew or Gentile. Notice that Paul here, as in Romans 9:1–5, stresses that Jesus the Messiah was a servant to Jews for the sake of the truth of God. By this he means so as to vindicate God's promises and prophecies given to the patriarchs, and in particular of course to Abraham, the forefather Paul spent a chapter talking about in Romans 4. But Christ also did what he did so that Gentiles might learn about the mercy of God (see Romans 11 and 12) and glorify God that his Son died even for the ungodly, the sinner, and even for his enemies.

To further make his point, Paul trots out four Old Testament texts that speak of Gentiles: 2 Samuel 22:50 coupled with Psalm 18:49, and then Deuteronomy 32:43, Psalm 117:1, and finally Isaiah 11:10 in the Septuagint (LXX) version. The point is, in part, to make clear that God had plans for the Gentiles all along, but what the first three quotations speak of is Jews praising God among the Gentiles, and then twice Gentiles praising the God of the Bible. This would seem to point rather clearly to Paul's desire that Jewish and

Gentile Christians praise God together in worship in Rome so that he could actually speak of the *ekklesia* in Rome. The last quotation in verse 12, however, has a different thrust. Here Paul stresses that the Messiah was raised up to rule over not just Israel but also the Gentile nations, and so the Gentiles should place their hope in him, not in emperors or current governmental officials. There may be an implicit critique here of placing too much faith in the Roman government, but nothing is alluded to here in regard to emperor worship, only that Christ is Lord over all.

The benediction in Romans 15:13 suggests that the God of hope wants to fill them with something they can really place their hope and trust in—namely, the joy and peace of God—and also the power of the Holy Spirit, which allows them to overflow with hope. Paul has, in fact, basically concluded his series of arguments directed largely at Gentile Christians in Rome, and what follows immediately is his peroration, as we shall see in tomorrow's lesson.

1. Why do you think there is so much emphasis on worship and praise here toward the conclusion of all Paul's arguments in Romans?

2. Why the direct appeal to these Gentile Christians to accept other Christians as they have been accepted?

3. In what areas today are you lacking in hope or peace? Consider journaling about these.

THREE

Return to Sender

Romans 15:14–22 *I myself am convinced, my brothers and sisters, that you yourselves are full of goodness, filled with knowledge and competent to instruct one another. [15]Yet I have written you quite boldly on some points to remind you of them again, because of the grace God gave me [16]to be a minister of Christ Jesus to the Gentiles. He gave me the priestly duty of proclaiming the gospel of God, so that the Gentiles might become an offering acceptable to God, sanctified by the Holy Spirit.*

[17]Therefore I glory in Christ Jesus in my service to God. [18]I will not venture to speak of anything except what Christ has accomplished through me in leading

the Gentiles to obey God by what I have said and done—¹⁹by the power of signs and wonders, through the power of the Spirit of God. So from Jerusalem all the way around to Illyricum, I have fully proclaimed the gospel of Christ. ²⁰It has always been my ambition to preach the gospel where Christ was not known, so that I would not be building on someone else's foundation. ²¹Rather, as it is written: "Those who were not told about him will see, and those who have not heard will understand."

²²This is why I have often been hindered from coming to you.

Understanding the Word. Here Paul returns to the themes he began with in chapter 1, about his own ministry, about the faith of the Romans and related matters that have been mentioned before. One type of peroration is a "recapitulation" and that is what we see here. Paul again flatters the audience, saying he believes they are full of goodness and Christian knowledge and ability to instruct one another, while at the same time stressing that he is the apostle to the Gentiles and he has a right, indeed a duty, to instruct them in this discourse, and later in person. Notice that in verses 16–17 Paul calls himself a "minister" (or "liturgist") (*leitourgos*) and a priest of the Gentiles. The former term means a religious official, and in particular says Paul is a priest who is supposed to proclaim the gospel of God so that the Gentiles might become an acceptable offering to God, presumably as living sacrifices sanctified by the Holy Spirit (see Romans 12:1). This is one of the very rare times Paul uses priestly language about the role he plays in relationship to Gentiles, strongly suggesting he has a necessary religious role to play in their lives. Notice that Paul says he has written to them "quite boldly" (verse 15), which is putting it mildly, partially in order to remind them of some things they already know, but clearly he tells them some things they've never likely heard before (e.g., Romans 11:25). This simply confirms that one of the major functions of Romans 1–8 was to build a theological foundation on common Christian grounds for what Paul was going to say in the rest of the discourse. Paul assumes that the audience has heard much of what he says in those first eight chapters before.

In verse 18, Paul begins to speak of what in particular he has done in "leading the Gentiles to obey God." More correctly, he is speaking of what Christ has done through him to lead Gentiles to that obedience. In a rarity, Paul speaks of his having performed miracles, something we hear about in Acts 13–20, but almost never in Paul's letters. The obedience of the Gentiles was in part brought about through God's shock-and-awe tactics through the powerful Spirit, by which Paul is referring to signs and wonders (i.e., miracles of various sorts, presumably mostly healings). Even more astounding than this is Paul's claim that he has fully proclaimed the gospel from Jerusalem all the way around to Illyricum, a city which today we would locate in former Yugoslavia or Albania. Paul is, of course, not claiming he has evangelized everywhere between these two cities, or even in these two specific cities. He is saying that he has done what God expected him to do in the eastern part of the Mediterranean and now he is hankering to go west where the gospel has not yet been proclaimed, by which he means Spain! Paul quotes Isaiah 52:15 of himself saying, in essence, that it was his task to go boldly where no one had gone before amongst the Gentiles to proclaim the gospel. That was his commission. The question this quotation and others that Paul applies to himself raises is: Did Paul see himself as the servant referred to in that Servant Song in Isaiah? The answer is perhaps so, as an extension of the ministry of Christ to the Gentiles.

The meaning of verse 22 is not completely clear. It seems to suggest that prior to the writing of this letter Paul had been hindered by God from coming to Rome (see the discussion on Romans 1) until Paul had finished the tasks God had assigned him between Jerusalem and Illyricum.

1. Was Paul a prophet and a miracle-worker, as well as an apostolic proclaimer of the gospel?

2. Why do you think God prevented Paul from coming to Rome not only until he had finished his tasks in the eastern empire, but for almost three more years after this letter was written?

3. Paul was faced with great delay in getting to Rome. Is there something that you are longing for which has not yet transpired?

FOUR

Go West, Old Man

Romans 15:23–29 *But now that there is no more place for me to work in these regions, and since I have been longing for many years to visit you, ²⁴I plan to do so when I go to Spain. I hope to see you while passing through and to have you*

assist me on my journey there, after I have enjoyed your company for a while.
²⁵Now, however, I am on my way to Jerusalem in the service of the Lord's people
there. ²⁶For Macedonia and Achaia were pleased to make a contribution for the
poor among the Lord's people in Jerusalem. ²⁷They were pleased to do it, and
indeed they owe it to them. For if the Gentiles have shared in the Jews' spiritual
blessings, they owe it to the Jews to share with them their material blessings. ²⁸So
after I have completed this task and have made sure that they have received this
contribution, I will go to Spain and visit you on the way. ²⁹I know that when I
come to you, I will come in the full measure of the blessing of Christ.

Understanding the Word. Finally Paul announces that he will come to Rome
on the way to Spain. His focus is on Spain, not Rome, and he uses the technical
language to make clear he doesn't intend to come to Rome and stay forever. He
speaks of having the Christians in Rome "assist [him] on [his] journey," which
is technical language for providing provisions and money to get him to his next
destination, Spain. We honestly do not know if he ever got there, due to his
legal problems that began to plague him after he wrote this letter. He says only
he hopes to come to Rome and enjoy their company for a while before moving
on westward. It is not clear what exactly Paul means when he says there is no
more room or place for his ministry in the eastern part of the Mediterranean,
but what is clear is Paul feels like he is done with that huge swath of territory except for one final task—he needs to go to deliver the collection taken
up from his Gentile churches for the saints in Jerusalem who needed famine
relief. Paul mentions only the churches in Macedonia and Achaia, but probably there were churches in Galatia and Asia as well that contributed to the
funds. It is not completely clear as to whether "the poor among God's people
in Jerusalem" are just Christians, or if this is a benevolence fund in general for
starving Jews back in Zion. In light of what Galatians 1–2 suggest, it seems
likely to be the former, and not the latter.

Paul is not implicitly soliciting funds from the Gentiles in Rome, but he
wants them to know that these other Gentile Christians were glad to give such
a benefaction to the Jerusalem church. Paul believes and probably emphasized
that they owed it to the mother church because they have shared in the spiritual blessings of the Messiah and the Jewish heritage and they should certainly
be willing to share material blessings with those who bequeathed them not
only the Scriptures, but also the Messiah and so their very salvation! Paul feels

he must go in person to deliver the collection and make sure it is received by the right people. And here we must mention that the rest of the record, including all of Paul's later letters, do not tell us exactly how it turned out, or whether it was well received. Acts 21 may imply it was received and used to pay for the vows of some Jewish Christians, but it is not completely clear or certain. Paul expresses confidence that when he comes to Rome he will come with the full blessing of Christ, by which he means presumably that he will have God's full blessing to head west, finally, having finished the work in the east.

1. Why is Paul so concerned about not building on other people's gospel work, but rather continuing to be a church planter on virgin soil?

2. What is the collection and why does Paul see it as so important?

3. Consider writing down today some key things you have learned during this study of Romans.

FIVE

Prayer Requests

Romans 15:30–33 RSV *I appeal to you, brethren, by our Lord Jesus Christ and by the love of the Spirit, to strive together with me in your prayers to God on my behalf, [31]that I may be delivered from the unbelievers in Judea, and that my service for Jerusalem may be acceptable to the saints, [32]so that by God's will I may come to you with joy and be refreshed in your company. [33]The God of peace be with you all. Amen.*

Understanding the Word. Paul speaks candidly at the end of chapter 15 about his struggles. He asks his audience to join him in his striving by praying with him for two crucial things: (1) that he might be kept safe from some unbelievers in Judaea whom might well want to do him in (it is even possible there was a contract out on Paul—see 2 Corinthians 11:24–26) and (2) that the collection will be favorably received. In fact, Paul had good reason to ask for prayers on both these matters as the account in Acts 21–22 makes evident. Paul himself will be praying fervently about these things, but he enlists the prayers of his new audience as well.

Paul wants to come to Rome with joy, and perhaps some relief in his heart, and he says he is looking forward to having his spirit refreshed while in Rome. He then asks that the God of peace be with the divided Christians in Rome.

1. What are the sorts of things Paul struggled with in his ministry?

2. Is there evidence that Paul had good reason to fear danger by returning to Jerusalem in person?

3. Sometimes it takes great vulnerability to share your struggles and ask others to pray for and with you. Is there something you feel the need to ask others to join you in prayer for? Consider taking action on that this week.

COMMENTARY NOTES

General Comments. Scholars who are experts in text criticism have long speculated about why it is that various manuscripts insert final doxologies and conclusions at the end of Romans 14, and chapters 15 and 16. One of the discussion topics in such debates has been as to whether Paul made two copies of this letter, one with, and one without chapter 16. A further speculation connected to this one is the idea that Romans with the chapter 16 ending was sent to Ephesus, rather than to Rome. These issues need to be considered one at a time.

First, it is entirely likely that Paul did make two copies of this lengthy document, but the normal practice would be to keep one copy for oneself, and send the other, not send out both copies, especially not send them out to two very different destinations. Second, despite older disclaimers, most scholars now realize that Romans is a situation-specific letter, especially from chapter 9 onward, and Paul would hardly be likely to send a situation-specific letter to two entirely separate destinations. Romans, unlike Ephesians, is most definitely not a circular letter. Third, there is the possibility that Paul sent two copies of this letter to Rome, one to the Gentile congregations, and one to the Jewish ones.

I am not much concerned with the various placements of the doxology or benediction because we know these letters were later part of the church liturgy, and then the lectionaries and the worship elements may have been added to or subtracted from various spots according to which bit of Romans was being read on a given Sunday. Romans 15 and 16 dealing with situation-specific travel and an exceedingly long list of greetings probably tended not to be used in early lectionaries and preaching, which would explain why we have a final doxology after Romans 14:23 in a whole variety of witnesses—A, P, 5, 33, 104 and in Armenian manuscripts, but also in L, various minuscule, and various Byzantine and Syriac manuscripts, and also in the West in the Old Latin in the Vulgate where you have Romans 1:1–14:23 plus 16:24 plus the doxology. In my estimation, scholars who think it likely Romans ended at the end of chapter 14 are not thinking through the later use of this material in worship, and the fact that chapters 15–16 do not particularly lend to general worship or preaching purposes in the ancient church. And then there is the issue of the heretic Marcion. He seems to have circulated copies of Romans in the second century without Romans 15–16 (see B. M. Metzger, *A Textual Commentary on the Greek New Testament, 2nd edition* 1994, pp. 470–73). In my estimation, there may have been two copies sent to Rome, or better, Romans 16 was originally a separate document, a letter of commendation for Phoebe and for Jewish Christians in Rome sent to the Gentile Christian majority, which would explain why in Papyrus 46 we find the doxology after Romans 15 but not at the end of Romans 16.

WEEK ELEVEN

GATHERING DISCUSSION OUTLINE

A. Open session in prayer.

B. View video for this week's readings.

C. What general impressions and thoughts do you have after considering the video and reading and the daily writings on these Scriptures?

D. Discuss questions based on the daily readings.

1. **KEY OBSERVATION:** Romans 15 makes very clear that Paul intended to send this letter, sail to Jerusalem, drop off the collection, and then come right to Rome, on the way to Spain.

   DISCUSSION QUESTION: In reading Acts 21:17–27:30, how did Paul actually make it to Rome? Is it likely he made it to Spain?

2. **KEY OBSERVATION:** Romans 15:4 provides us with an interesting glimpse of Paul's view of Scripture and how it functions for Christians.

   DISCUSSION QUESTION: What uses does Paul say the Old Testament Scripture has for Christians?

3. **KEY OBSERVATION:** Throughout chapter 15 Paul quotes heavily from the Old Testament.

   DISCUSSION QUESTION: What is Paul communicating through the Old Testament quotations he uses in 15:7–13?

4. **KEY OBSERVATION:** Paul speaks candidly at the end of chapter 15 about his struggles and solicits prayers from his audience.

   DISCUSSION QUESTION: How would Paul's request for prayer help to strengthen his message of unity to his audience?

5. **KEY OBSERVATION:** One of the things that Romans 15 shows us is that even the plans of an apostle like Paul could go awry.

   DISCUSSION QUESTION: What lesson can we learn from Paul's experience?

E. What facts and information presented in the commentary portion of the lesson help you understand the weekly Scripture?

F. Close session with prayer.

WEEK TWELVE

Romans 16:1–27

Postcards from the Edge (of the Empire)

INTRODUCTION

On first blush you may be wondering, *Why are we studying all these names?* People tend to ignore or overlook the conclusion of Romans, but to do so is to ignore altogether the importance of Paul's social network for his ministry. Paul, as this passage demonstrates, had a lot of connections, a lot of friends, and a lot of coworkers. He was not the Lone Ranger for Jesus, as he is sometimes depicted. This chapter details for us some of these relationships and it tells us volumes about some of the people who were with Paul and some who are already in Rome. In some cases we are told more, in some cases less, but all of this material is revealing of the character of early Christianity, and actually whole books have been written based on Romans 16! What do we really know about the church that already existed in Rome before either Paul, or apparently Peter, got there (noting that Peter is nowhere mentioned in this chapter or elsewhere in Romans)?

We know that the church had existed a considerable period of time by the time this letter was penned in about AD 57. Indeed, it had been going so long that Paul for years had been intending to come visit, but had been hindered by the need to finish the work in the eastern end of the empire first. What Acts 2 suggests is that there were Jewish converts at Pentecost in AD 30 who were from Rome and took the gospel back to Rome with them. If so, the church had been going for twenty-seven years by the time Paul wrote Romans.

Sometimes silences are pregnant. You will notice that Paul, in Romans, unlike in, say, Philippians, does not address a leadership group who are leading the largely Gentile churches in Rome. He will mention leaders in Romans 16 but these are his Jewish Christian coworkers now in Rome. It would appear there was no apostle who founded the churches in Rome. It seems to have been founded not by a Peter or a Paul but by pilgrims from the eastern part of the empire who came to Rome, or already lived in Rome, and planted the gospel there.

It is remarkable that Paul knows and is able to name some twenty-six persons in Romans 16, and he stresses his close personal relationship with quite a few of these persons—Andronicus, Junia, and Herodion are said to be Paul's own relatives. At a minimum, this means they are Jewish Christians, but it may also mean they are close kin to Paul. Prisca/Priscilla, Aquila, and Urbanus are all called Paul's coworkers, not in Rome since he hasn't been there yet, nor as an advance guard that Paul has sent to Rome. Rather they had worked with Paul back east. Paul also calls those with Philologus "saints," a usual code word for Jewish Christians. As we shall see, at least sixteen of the twenty-six are singled out in some special way, using honorific terms. This is no ordinary greeting card; it is more like an honor roll.

Various scholars have suggested that Paul is referring to people who were expelled from Rome by the Emperor Claudius and had returned after Claudius's death in AD 54. This, in turn, surely means all those listed here are Jewish Christians who are named in detail because Paul wants them all personally embraced and honored by the Gentile Christians, and incorporated into their fellowship. Note that at least twelve of the twenty-six are spoken of in a way that necessitates the conclusion that they had encountered and, in some cases, worked with Paul in the east previously. Some, like Andronicus and Junia, had been in jail with Paul, and some, like Priscilla and Aquila, had been his frequent coworkers in various cities. Paul, in this chapter, is working hard to unite the divided Christians in Rome before he gets there.

Finally, the rhetorical effect of this listing in Romans 16 is considerable: (1) it makes clear that the Gentile Christians in Rome can no longer ignore or claim to not know about these people; (2) it shows that Paul does have sources in Rome, indeed a large social network; (3) the rhetorical function of the special descriptions and honorific titles given to those named is to make clear they are important hardworking Christians in whose debt the Gentile Christians in Rome are, whether they ever knew this before this letter was written or not; (4) it is not an accident that only here in Romans in verse 16 do we have global greetings from all the Pauline churches of the east. The point is that all eyes of the churches are turning to Rome, as Paul is, and here is a reminder that the Roman church is part of a much larger network of churches. This is also why Paul requested prayer for himself as he returns to Jerusalem.

ONE

Phoebe, the First Deacon

Romans 16:1–2 *I commend to you our sister Phoebe, a deacon of the church in Cenchreae. ²I ask you to receive her in the Lord in a way worthy of his people and to give her any help she may need from you, for she has been the benefactor of many people, including me.*

Understanding the Word. Women and their religious roles varied from one subculture to another in the Roman Empire. On the one hand, there were no Jewish priestesses. On the other hand, there were plenty of Greco-Roman ones, not to mention oracles, vestal virgins, and a host of other roles. Long story short, lots of Gentile women played important religious roles in Paul's world, and even some Jewish women seem to have done so as well, especially in the Diaspora. It should not then come as a shock that Paul has various female coworkers in ministry who play a variety of roles. We will meet some of the most important ones in Romans 16.

Phoebe is commended to the audience in Rome, and immediately described as a sister and a deacon in the church in Cenchreae, the eastern port city of Corinth. Notice Paul says "our sister," indicating all Christians everywhere are part of the same family of God, they are all brothers and sisters to each other and should be treated as family. Here is actually the first known reference to someone holding the office of deacon, and the reference is clearly to a woman. We probably hear of women serving this way also in 1 Timothy 2:8–13. We are not sure of what the total scope was of the role of a deacon at this juncture, but the term itself suggests practical service as *diakonia* in its root meaning "refers to waiting on tables." When coupled with some of the other terms Paul uses here, it may mean a reasonable well-to-do woman who provides such practical service, and the use of the word *ousan* with the term "deacon" suggests an ongoing ministry.

Ironically enough it is at Romans 16:1 that we have our very first reference to the *ekklesia* but not in Rome, not in that place where Christians are so divided along largely ethnic lines. No, Paul is referring to the church in Cenchreae where Phoebe serves, and probably where Paul is currently, from which port he will sail east to Jerusalem.

Paul requests that the Gentile Christians in Rome receive Phoebe warmly, in a way worthy of God's people, "and give her any help she may need." Literally the text says "welcome her in the Lord, worthy of the saints," which suggests she is among the saints, which in turn suggests (see Romans 15 and the reference to the saints in Jerusalem who are needy) she is a Jewish Christian, like Paul. The latter phrase "give her help" suggests Phoebe is not merely planning on passing through Rome, but rather is coming to do some practical ministry there. I would suggest as well that she is probably Paul's vanguard, going ahead of him to Rome to prepare the way, even to prepare a place for him, and probably she is the bearer (and reader of) this letter to the Romans, hence placing her first in this list and commending her especially.

Paul then calls Phoebe a *prostatis*. If you look at the cognate term in Romans 12:8 this suggests that the word means someone in charge of some practical service, or charitable work, which also comports with calling her a deacon. She would be a leader in some sort of caregiving work. If we take the term at face value it means something like "protector" or "benefactor" or "patroness." We have two Jewish inscriptions in Rome where the term has the latter sense (CIJ 100, 365). There is evidence, as well, of Jewish women being patronesses and benefactors of Diaspora synagogues too [see my Romans commentary, *Paul's Letter to the Romans*, (Eerdmans, 2004)]. But a further clue comes from the fact that Paul regularly designates the collection as a *diakonia*, and so it would appear that here Paul is saying that Phoebe has been the financial agent and patroness of Paul himself as well as others. What is especially striking about this is that Paul had rejected patronage from some in Corinth, and had in engaged in making tents, in order to avoid the appearance of being a paid speaker of a patron and to avoid entangling alliances. This suggests that Paul does not fear that Phoebe will treat him as if he were merely her client. It is possible she provided Paul with some shelter as well once the troubles started in Corinth (cf. Acts 18:18). If she has been the patroness of many, she is likely a rather wealthy person. Paul had no problems working with a high-status person, and indeed converting at least some of those sorts of people was crucial in any given town or city, as they were the ones likely to be able to provide a private venue where Christians could assemble and worship and have fellowship.

1. What does it tell you about Paul's view of women's roles in the church that he commends a woman as the first deacon he has ever mentioned, and trusts her enough probably to have her deliver the letter to the Romans in person?

2. Why was it important, practically speaking, for Paul to convert at least some high-status persons to the faith?

3. Here we see Phoebe utilizing her gifts in service to the church. In what ways are you engaging your gifts in service to the church?

TWO

Priscilla and Aquila, Paul's Coworkers

Romans 16:3–5 *Greet Priscilla and Aquila, my co-workers in Christ Jesus.* *⁴They risked their lives for me. Not only I but all the churches of the Gentiles are grateful to them.*

⁵Greet also the church that meets at their house.

Greet my dear friend Epenetus, who was the first convert to Christ in the province of Asia.

Understanding the Word. Besides Timothy, and perhaps Titus, Priscilla and Aquila appear to have been Paul's most long-running coworkers, and it should be noticed that almost always Priscilla is named first. Since Paul does not follow the dictums of social status in ranking people, it is probable that if anyone took the lead among that ministry couple in helping Paul, it was Priscilla. When one reads, for example, the story of the instruction of Apollos about Christian baptism in Acts 18, the text is quite clear to mention Priscilla first (verse 26). In 1 Corinthians 16:19 we hear about the church, which meets in the house of Priscilla and Aquila in Ephesus. Here in Romans 16 we catch up with them living in Rome. Corinth. Ephesus. Rome. These are traveling missionaries working closely with Paul and establishing house churches wherever they go.

No wonder Paul gives them pride of place here and says, "my co-workers." He adds that they had risked their very lives for Paul's sake. And this brings us to the word used here for greeting.

Aspazomai does not merely mean "greet" in some perfunctory way. It literally means to wrap one's arms around somebody and embrace them, and notice it is sometimes accompanied with the command to offer a "holy kiss" as well (verse 16). In other words, it means greet with every show of warmth and affection like you would a close family member. Remember that Paul is giving this exhortation to the Gentile Christians in Rome, and now they are being commanded to embrace the Jewish Christians in Rome that Paul will list. They are to be welcomed into the homes, the inner circles, the sanctums of these Gentile Christians. Paul is going all out to create a new social ethos amongst Roman Christians. Notice as well that Paul usually sends greetings to an audience, but here he is commanding a group of people *in the audience* to warmly receive another group of people in Rome! This is not merely unusual in Paul's letters, it is unprecedented and it relates to the special dysfunctional situation in Rome where there is no single united group that could be called *ekklesia* there.

It should also be remembered that Paul also shared a trade with Priscilla and Aquila, according to Acts 18. They all made tents out of goat's hair cloth, called *cilicium*, after Paul's native region, Cilicia, which was famous for making such items. The decision to make tents in Corinth was not a random one, but in part a good business decision, because the Isthmian games were held nearby every two years, and most of the attendees from out of town needed to rent a tent. More important, if we ask how Paul, as well as his parents, could have become a Roman citizen I would suggest it was from making tents, and selling them to the Roman army stationed in and near Tarsus. Citizenship was regularly granted to those providing a service to the empire.

It's almost like piling on when Paul finally adds in verse 4, "all the churches of the Gentiles are grateful to them" by which he surely means "all the other churches" and the not-so-subtle implication is, the Gentile church in Rome should start showing it as well! Paul is about as subtle as a bag of hammers. Finally, in verse 5 Paul mentions that the church, which meets in Priscilla and Aquila's house, should all be greeted by the Roman Gentile Christians. This apparently includes Epenetus, the first convert in the province of Asia, who is not staying in Rome, and is a good friend of Paul's. There was going to be a whole lot of hugging of Jews going on if Paul was obeyed in Rome.

1. What trade did Paul share in common with Priscilla and Aquila?

2. What do you make of the verb *aspazomai*? Would the translation of British scholar J. B. Philips, "greet one another with a hardy handshake," really get at what Paul was calling for?

3. Consider the phrase "greet with every show of warmth and affection like you would a close family member. What would have to change in your church (or home) for people to be embraced with this kind of hospitality?

THREE

Greetings of Apostles, Coworkers, and Relatives

Romans 16:6–16 *Greet Mary, who worked very hard for you.*

[7]Greet Andronicus and Junia, my fellow Jews who have been in prison with me. They are outstanding among the apostles, and they were in Christ before I was.

[8]Greet Ampliatus, my dear friend in the Lord.

[9]Greet Urbanus, our co-worker in Christ, and my dear friend Stachys.

[10]Greet Apelles, whose fidelity to Christ has stood the test.

Greet those who belong to the household of Aristobulus.

[11]Greet Herodion, my fellow Jew.

Greet those in the household of Narcissus who are in the Lord.

[12]Greet Tryphena and Tryphosa, those women who work hard in the Lord.

Greet my dear friend Persis, another woman who has worked very hard in the Lord.

[13]Greet Rufus, chosen in the Lord, and his mother, who has been a mother to me, too.

[14]Greet Asyncritus, Phlegon, Hermes, Patrobas, Hermas and the other brothers and sisters with them.

¹⁵Greet Philologus, Julia, Nereus and his sister, and Olympas and all the Lord's people who are with them.
¹⁶Greet one another with a holy kiss.
All the churches of Christ send greetings.

Understanding the Word. First of all, we need to notice that every one of the greetings in this section involves the imperative "greet [with every show of affections]." All of them. Second, in some cases individuals are mentioned, but in some cases "those in the household of X," which leads to the suggestion that Paul is greeting people by household groups, or house churches as we might call them, where possible. Third, at least eight of these people are women. In some cases, it is possible that "those in the household of X" suggests that the head of the household is not a Christian, and that we are talking about subordinate members of a household, perhaps especially some slaves or domestic servants. There may also be some famous Christians listed as well. We will start with them.

Herodion is listed as Paul's fellow Jew in verse 11. This is, of course, a variant of the name Herod. We need to connect this with the reference to Aristobolus in verse 10, as it has been suggested he, too, was a member of the family of Herod. In fact, there was a grandson of Herod the Great and a brother of Herod Agrippa I who had this name. Josephus says he went to Rome in the 40s with Herod Agrippa I to get an education. The name Aristobolus is a rare one, so it seems unlikely this is someone else, especially when listed next to someone named Herodion. Herodion was likely a freedman from the family of Herod. We must assume that Paul knew these people in Judaea and that, in the case of Herodion, he became a Christian and, in the case of Aristobolus, some members of his household became Christians in Rome. It would appear that Jewish Christians in Rome evangelized their own people, and tried to otherwise maintain a low profile, especially after the banishment of various leaders by Claudius.

Notice in verse 13 the reference to Rufus, and "his mother who has been a mother to me, too." There is a Rufus (which is a Latin name) mentioned in Mark 15:21 who is the son of Simon of Cyrene. It is possible this is the same person, because Mark's gospel was probably written to Christians in Rome, in which case both men named Rufus in the New Testament are connected to the same place. Paul says his mother has been a mother to Paul, and this surely must have transpired elsewhere, perhaps in Judaea. Imagine being "mothered" by the wife of the person who carried Jesus' cross! She must have had some tales to tell, as likely did Rufus. Here he is called "the chosen (or elect) in the Lord." We do not know what he was chosen especially to do.

Notice that three of the four people that Paul has said worked hard for the Roman Christians are women. Notice too these female names—Maria, Tryphaena, Tryphosa, and Persis. For some reason Paul only uses the verb *kopiao*, which refers to hard work, of the women in this whole list in Romans 16. Possibly these women had more time to devote to Christian service. It seems likely that the Tryphaena and Tryphosa are slaves, because they have slave nicknames meaning dainty and delicate! Was Christianity spread to a great extent in Rome by slaves and perhaps especially female slaves? Persis is also a popular slave name and in the RSV she is called "beloved," presumably by her fellow Jewish Christians. But now we come to the biggest surprise.

Consider what Paul says about Andronicus and Junia in verse 7: (1) they are Paul's fellow Jews, perhaps even close kin; (2) they have been in prison with Paul, meaning of course they have worked with him closely; (3) they are noteworthy or outstanding among the apostles. Note that this is not to be translated "noteworthy (or outstanding) *to* the apostles." The preposition *en*, which means "in" or "among" is unlikely to be used to express "to the apostles"; (4) "and they were in Christ before [Paul]." Now we need to think about this very carefully. These persons became Christians before Paul did, which is to say before AD 35 or so. Paul was converted less than a decade after Jesus' death in AD 30. Where would this ministry couple have had to have been to be converted before there even was an apostle to the Gentiles? The answer is in Jerusalem or Judaea, or less likely Damascus or Antioch. Nowhere else had the gospel spread at so early a date, at least not intentionally.

Second, Paul is perfectly happy to call both of these persons apostles. While it is true that the term *apostle* can mean a missionary of a particular church (see 2 Corinthians 8–9), the way that sort of person was distinguished was precisely by calling them an "apostle of X church." Nothing like that is said about Andronicus and Junia, and besides, they were surely not imprisoned with Paul in Jerusalem and Judaea at some early date. And this leads to the biggest surprise of all. The Latin name Junia is the simple equivalent of the Jewish name Joanna. Is it possible that this "Joanna" is the one referred to in Luke's gospel as one of the original female disciples of Jesus? The answer is yes. Indeed, I would say it is more than possible, it is likely. When Paul uses the term "apostle" without the qualifier "of this or that church," he is referring to someone like himself who has seen the risen Lord. It is suggested in 1 Corinthians 9:1–2 that this was, in Paul's mind, the essential criteria for being an apostle—one had to have seen the risen Lord. Notice the way Paul talks about this in 1 Corinthians 15, saying he is the very last and least of the apostles, in part because he is the last to have seen the risen Lord. Again, if we ask, where would Junia have had to have been to have seen the risen Lord and become an apostle? The answer is either Judaea or Galilee, and probably the former. We have a clear account in Luke 24 of women, including Joanna, going to the tomb, seeing the angels, and then, with Mary Magdalene (see Matthew 28:10), seeing the risen Jesus.

So what happened to the high-status woman who was the wife of Herod's estate agent, Chuza, but chose to become a follower of Jesus all over Galilee and to Judaea and Jerusalem as well (see Luke 8:1–3)? In early Judaism, a man could simply write out a bill of divorce on the spot. Jewish women were generally not able to do this. Remember that Herod Antipas was the enemy of and the one who beheaded Jesus' cousin John the Baptizer. He cannot have been pleased that the wife of his estate agent was traipsing around Galilee and elsewhere, and even providing provisions for the band of disciples and Jesus. Chuza had to choose between his job and his wife in all likelihood. A woman who wandered around with a man she was not related to would be a scandal in that society. Thus, it is highly likely that Joanna was divorced by the time Jesus' ministry ended in Jerusalem, and at some juncture she remarried another Jewish Christian who had seen the Lord—Andronicus. We have no additional information about him. What we can say is that there appear to be two prominent figures in early Christianity who were once traveling disciples with Jesus, and went on to have extensive missionary ministries outside the Holy Land—Peter and Joanna.

1. Why does Paul keep commending his fellow Jewish Christians whom he is close to?

2. What does this list tell you about Paul's view of women doing various sorts of ministries, including apostolic ministries?

3. We have considered Paul's view of women having various (and prominent) roles in ministry. How is this shaping/changing/encouraging your views?

FOUR

The Peroration for Jewish Christians

Romans 16:17–20 *I urge you, brothers and sisters, to watch out for those who cause divisions and put obstacles in your way that are contrary to the teaching you have learned. Keep away from them. ¹⁸For such people are not serving our Lord Christ, but their own appetites. By smooth talk and flattery they deceive the minds of naive people. ¹⁹Everyone has heard about your obedience, so I rejoice because of you; but I want you to be wise about what is good, and innocent about what is evil.*

²⁰The God of peace will soon crush Satan under your feet.
The grace of our Lord Jesus be with you.

Understanding the Word. The final peroration, found here in 16:17–20, speaks further about and into the situation of the divisions in the Roman church between the weak and the strong, between the Jewish Christians and the Gentiles. Here there is a stern warning to watch out for those who are promoters of or direct causes of divisions, which puts obstacles in the way of obeying the call to unity and concord that Paul has been giving in this letter. He points out that this call was already a part of the teaching they have had in the past, and presumably he knows this from some of his coworkers in Rome.

Here, we have a picking up of some of the exhortations in Romans 14 where we heard about people who were too scrupulous about their food, and alternately about those who were violating the consciences of the scrupulous by focusing on satisfying their own appetites. Paul adds that the latter, who apparently have been trying to persuade the weak, have used smooth talk and flattery so as to deceive the minds of naive Christians, and this in itself is a serious sin. The attempt to make everyone like what you like, eat what you eat, and so on is an attempt to recreate others in your own image, a serious sin. Paul adds however that "everyone," presumably meaning the other largely Gentile churches, has heard of their obedience to the gospel previously, but going forward he is warning against listening to the siren song of the strong and to "be wise about what is good, and innocent about what is evil," a variant of Jesus' teaching about being wise as serpents and innocent as doves (see Matthew 10:16).

The peroration closes with a promise. "The God of peace will soon crush Satan under your feet." Notice that the Greek has a definite article before the word "Satan." The term is not a name but a title—the Adversary. Perhaps the remembering of the saying of Jesus about serpents and doves prompted Paul to think of the garden story about the serpent, and the curse on the snake warning of the crushing of him under the feet of Eve's descendants (see Genesis 3:14–15). Yet here it is God in person who will demolish Satan, not the believers. Probably the Greek phrase *en taxei* modifies the verb "crush" here and means "quickly," though it could certainly be "soon," in which case Paul would likely be referring to the crushing of the sources of divisions between the Jewish and Gentile Christians in Rome.

In any case, this peroration unveils what we have already seen evidence of in this letter—divisions in the body of Christ in Rome, and Paul's attempt to heal the breach between Jew and Gentile, weak and strong in Christ.

1. What caused the divisions in the Roman Christian community?

2. Who does Paul place the onus on to fix the problem, humanly speaking?

3. When you see or hear of divisions in your local church, what do you think your response could be?

FIVE

Final Greetings from Corinth

Romans 16:21–27 RSV *Timothy, my fellow worker, greets you; so do Lucius and Jason and Sosip'ater, my kinsmen.*
²²I Tertius, the writer of this letter, greet you in the Lord.

²³*Ga´ius, who is host to me and to the whole church, greets you. Eras´tus, the city treasurer, and our brother Quartus, greet you.*

²⁵*Now to him who is able to strengthen you according to my gospel and the preaching of Jesus Christ, according to the revelation of the mystery which was kept secret for long ages ²⁶but is now disclosed and through the prophetic writings is made known to all nations, according to the command of the eternal God, to bring about the obedience of faith—²⁷to the only wise God be glory for evermore through Jesus Christ! Amen.*

Understanding the Word. The final greetings do not involve exhortations to anyone in Rome, but are more like Paul's normal greetings in other letters, in this case from other Christians with Paul in Corinth or its port of Cenchreae. Timothy, perhaps Paul's closest coworker and a person whom later he calls his son (1 Timothy 1:18), sends greetings as do three other Christians whom Paul notes are all Jewish Christians, like Paul and Timothy. These may be some of the same persons mentioned in Acts 20:4, but it seems unlikely that Lucius is the same person as Luke.

Verse 22 is important in several regards, not least because it makes clear Paul definitely used scribes in the writing of these long letter discourses. Here it was Tertius who did the arduous task, and sends greeting to those in Rome, perhaps especially all of these greetings are directed to those they already knew who came from Corinth, folks such as Priscilla and Aquila. Then there is the reference to Gaius, who has been providing some hospitality for Paul and indeed for the whole church that meets in his house, so it seems likely Paul has been staying with Gaius rather than Phoebe.

Even more interesting is the second half of verse 23 where Erastus, the city treasurer (or in NIV, director of public works) sends greetings along with Quartus. This Erastus is surely the same person as the Erastus mentioned in a paving stone discovered in front of the amphitheater in Corinth during a 1929 archeological excavation. The paving stone dates to before AD 50 and says, "Erastus, in return for his aedileship laid [the pavement] at his own expense." *Aedile* was indeed the officer of public workers or the city treasurer, and what we are being told in the inscription is that Erastus did a public service while running for office, in order to show his honor and good-will and using his own money to make clear he was fit for this very office. His mention here reminds us again that Paul converted various high-status persons in various cities, who became important advocates for and protectors of Christians in those cities. One imagines that Erastus ran into Paul in the shops in Corinth making tents, and having come to collect the rent as city treasurer, he got something more valuable than he bargained for from Paul—the gospel.

The final doxology in verses 25–27 is rich and full of meaning. Paul says that God is able to establish the Christians in Rome on a solid footing, and he stresses that this is in accord with the revelation of the mysterious plan of God for Gentiles and Jews all along. This mystery Paul has unveiled in Romans 11 about the salvation of the full number of the Gentiles and then of all Israel as well, but all in God's good time and timing. This plan was already intimated in the Old Testament, perhaps especially in Isaiah 40–66 on which Paul often relies, and indeed it will come to pass because the eternal God has commanded it. Once more here at the end Paul stresses that what God wanted all along was the Gentiles, like the Jews, to believe in, honor, and worship the one true God. And to become obedient to the gospel that Paul preached—an obedience that comes through faith in the right God, the righteous God, the righteousness of God. To that "only wise God," Paul concludes this magnificent discourse with praise, indeed saying glory be to that God forever and ever. Amen.

1. What do we learn about Paul's circumstances and living situation in or near Corinth from these verses?

2. What is the long hidden mystery, foretold in the Scriptures and now revealed in human history?

3. How would you summarize what you have learned in this study? Consider writing what you have come to understand about Romans into a paragraph, then a sentence, or even just a few words.

COMMENTARY NOTES

General Comments. Paul's social network is revealed for all to see in Romans 16. One of the obvious things at the beginning and end of this chapter is that Paul relied on higher-status persons of some means to further the cause of the gospel. He had both well-to-do patrons and patronesses, and he stayed in the homes of those who could also house a group of Christians for their meetings. If you want to get a better sense of this, see my brief work of historical fiction, *A Week in the Life of Corinth* (InterVarsity Press, 2012).

Day 1, verse 1. The term *diakonia* and its cognates *diakonos* and the verb *diakoneo* deserve to be studied together. The verb means "to serve or wait on," or it can mean "to provide for" or even "to care for." The noun has the simple sense of a servant, and the masculine term can be used of both male and female servants. Here it is important not to call Phoebe a deaconess for the very good reason that there was not an order of deaconesses for another three hundred years in church history. Interestingly, an inscription has been found on the Mount of Olives speaking of a woman named Sophia who is a deaconess and is called "the second

Phoebe" (see Witherington and Hyatt, *Paul's Letter to the Romans*, pp. 382–83).

Day 3, verse 7. Sometimes, in older translations, some have suggested that the name Junia is actually Junias, a man's name. There are a whole series of problems with this, and frankly the suggestion is made in order to avoid calling a woman an apostle. First of all, Junia is a female Roman deity. You did not name men after a goddess! This would be like a boy named Sue. Second, there is absolutely no support in literary texts or in ancient inscriptions for the name Junias, but the name Junia is incredibly common. So, yes, with a high degree of certainty we can say that a woman named Junia is called an apostle. Another artful dodge of the facts is the attempt to make the phrase in question ("outstanding among the apostles") mean "esteemed by the apostles." Unfortunately for that suggestion the phrase "in [*en* in Greek] the apostles" is not the way one would say "by the apostles" in Greek. There is a perfectly good Greek word that means "by" and it is *apo* not *en*. In a case like this, grammar definitely matters. Andronicus and Junia were yet another ministry couple, like Priscilla and Aquila who worked with Paul.

WEEK TWELVE

GATHERING DISCUSSION OUTLINE

A. Open session in prayer.

B. View video for this week's readings.

C. What general impressions and thoughts do you have after considering the video and reading and the daily writings on these Scriptures?

D. Discuss questions based on the daily readings.

    1. **KEY OBSERVATION:** Romans 16 is certainly easy to overlook in view of all the rich material that comes before it, but there is no passage in the Pauline letters that is more revealing about the character of early Christian ministry in Pauline form than this one.

    DISCUSSION QUESTION: What has been your experience in the past in reading Romans 16? Have you ever given any thought to the names listed?

    2. **KEY OBSERVATION:** It seems quite likely that Junia is the same person as Joanna who was a disciple of Jesus in Galilee and Judaea, and was one of the women who were last at the cross, first at the tomb, and first to see the risen Jesus.

    DISCUSSION QUESTION: Do you think Junia and Joanna could be the same person?

    3. **KEY OBSERVATION:** Paul's social network is revealed for all to see in Romans 16.

DISCUSSION QUESTION: What new insights have you gained about Paul's social network through this study of Romans 16?

4. **KEY OBSERVATION:** In this passage, we get a sense that Christianity was spread in part by slaves, and some of them perhaps imperial slaves.

   DISCUSSION QUESTION: How do you think slaves would have spread the gospel?

5. **KEY OBSERVATION:** In chapter 16 Paul comes across as a person who thinks God is very concerned that the Jewish Christians in Rome are struggling and need to be embraced by the Gentile Christians.

   DISCUSSION QUESTION: What does Paul say will happen to those who are making things difficult for the Jewish Christians? How will they be dealt with?

E. What facts and information presented in the commentary portion of the lesson help you understand the weekly Scripture?

F. Close session with prayer.